PORTRAIT OF
EDITH WHARTON

PERCY LUBBOCK

PORTRAIT OF
EDITH WHARTON

New York and London

APPLETON-CENTURY-CROFTS, INC.

PREFACE

in a letter to G. Lapsley

———

My dear Gaillard,

It is nearly seven years since you and I sat together on an Italian terrace, discussing the book that as Edith Wharton's literary executor you had asked me to write about her. What kind of book should it be? Certainly not a formal biography, the 'Life and Letters of Mrs. Wharton'; her own *Backward Glance*, informal as it is, seemed biography enough; and though it might not be difficult to make a collection of her letters, she was not one to whom letter-writing was a natural overflow of herself and her talk—her letters would give no living picture of her, to speak for itself. The book then, the book we were discussing, must be a portrait, a likeness of her as her friends knew her and as she lives in their memory: we were agreed on that. And another point: in a book of this kind any critical handling of her own books would be out of place; they would only appear, so to speak, as her own, in association with her, and there would be no attempt to take them from her and deal with them as ours, the possession of us all. We still agreed; but I began to discover difficulties. Well as I knew her and much as I saw of her during many years, they were only the years of a part of her life; of my own knowledge I knew nothing of her American life and its background, and far too little of the host of

[v]

friends on both sides of the ocean who peopled her world—far too little, that is, to place her among them in the abundance of their company; and how should a portrait of Edith Wharton give a true likeness if it failed to show her encompassed by the troops of her friends? Could the want be in any way supplied? It might be to some extent if her friends would help; and you undertook to ask for the help of as many as could be reached, of those who were left. The result was generous help from many quarters—in the form of recollections, reflections, notes of all kinds—freely placed at my disposal to be used in any manner that should accord with the design of the book: for a design it must have, single and strict, if it was to be what *she* would call a book, and to her of all people we could not dedicate an assembly of stray leaves, calling it a book. On the help thus provided I have, as you will see, drawn very freely—more freely indeed than you will see, though I have acknowledged my debts wherever I could; and yet, if a book was to be made of it, my book was bound, do what I might, to show the limitations of a single point of view, and to many of her friends its limitations will be only too obvious. But we discussed all this and agreed that they were inevitable, and so they will be no surprise to you; and still I hope that when you see her in what follows you will recognise our friend.

What we neither of us foreboded, as we talked on that terrace, was that it would be seven years before the book was in your hands. But of the load of history under which it has crouched in the interval I need scarcely speak. And here it is at last.

PERCY LUBBOCK

Montreux
September, 1944

Contents

Contents

PORTRAIT OF
EDITH WHARTON

I

At first sight

Before she settled in Europe she used to flash upon England at intervals, and her coming was always heralded by what Henry James called 'urgent and terrible signals,' directed upon Lamb House. She seemed to regard him, not only as the master of her art but as the master of her ceremonies too, when she planned a descent upon our island, and he was warned for duty. It was a great office and privilege, no doubt; but he had just established himself at Rye for a season of secluded work, and now he was called upon for action, for a readjustment of his life to meet her terms, and there was no time for due thought to be taken; she was already upon the sea, with her husband and her motor-car and the rest of her retinue; she had disembarked, she was at his door. There were large enfolding embraces, there was a great phrase of opulent welcome that rolled out to greet her; but almost before he knew where he was or had surmounted his climax she had plucked him forth, seated him beside her in the chariot of fire and whirled him away. It was magnificent, it was Napoleonic; but how little she understood the life of the literary hermit, its dedication to solitude and silence, its sacrifice to its task! She a writer, a novelist, a colleague of the great old craft?

—she .was a dazzling intruder, *la femme fatale,* the golden pheasant invading the barnyard; she was all that only his eloquence could depict, but she was not an easy guest for a quiet house, where the typewriter daily clacked and tinkled through the long hours and mazes of dictation. However, there she was, the dear great lady to whom none said nay; she had broken up his days and scattered his plans and devoured his expostulations, and they were off.

Such, if you listened to Henry James, was the manner of her impact upon our shore in those old days, now a long generation ago, and it is not to be denied that as a guest she was a handful. But though his cries resounded, his surrender was whole-hearted when he made it, and he was a magnanimous captive. Indeed there was nothing else for it; she knew her mind, she made her own plans and chose her own company; there was no way open but to follow her. To tell the truth he was not sorry to follow her away from Lamb House, to escort her on her flight and to place her securely under another roof. The wild woman, angel of devastation, when someone else was responsible for her he could enjoy her society without a care—and nowhere more freely, more expansively, than under the roof of Howard Sturgis at Windsor, home of hospitality ever open, prepared with its widest and tenderest embrace for these two. Nobody, not the fatal woman herself, could catch Howard at a disadvantage; he was ready for all and for everything with the wit and warmth and freedom of his bounty. His house was delivered into her hands; and there could be no better moment for a first sight of the interesting intruder than this, when she takes the place of honour between the pair of them, Howard and Henry, at Queen's Acre. Together they gave her, each after his manner, very different the one from the other, the perfect condition for enjoyment, and when she enjoyed herself in talk with them she showed it. She didn't pay great attention to anyone else, but she could be forgiven for this, where she sat; and there were other eyes upon her, making the most of their chance.

So there she is—sitting very upright and straight-backed, but all alive, easy and active in repose; clothed with much elegance, expensive in her neatness—fitted into her raiment, if I may so put it, with rounded precision, with nothing that strays or exceeds, but everything of the best; her head held high, and her red-brown hair, very pretty and fine, dressed with accurate art; and her face, not a young face at all, rather worn and reticulated, in spite of the youth of her figure and movement, and not a striking or a strongly marked face, nor one that told much of herself, if it weren't for the quick light in her eye and the flash of her glance: there she is then, the rare creature of whom Howard and Henry have so often talked, and now we see her at last. Clear-cut, finely finished and trimmed and edged as she was, yet she seemed to bring a great deal with her and to occupy the space about her as one well used to plenty of space. What she brought with her might appear, I must own, a little estranging at first, at least to those whom she didn't particularly notice; for she brought the world, and she was so much at her ease in it, so naturally at home there, that the old everyday life seemed to vanish as she took possession. It was a brilliant world, no doubt the very best, if that is the world you like; but it was a sudden change—it might be disconcerting at first, and no wonder; like the poor man in the Arabian tale, you might look round in a daze for your old shabby comforts of last night. However—she sat there in her circle of light, upon the scene transformed, and there was shade beyond it to protect an observer. It was clear, and this was a disappointment, that those in the shade couldn't hope to attract her interest; but at any rate there was plenty to observe.

With Henry and Howard on either side of her she hadn't a moment to lose; she seized the hour for such a play of talk with two such talkers, both giving her their best. It was for Henry to begin. He began, as usual, long before he reached his beginning; and she watched and waited, on the edge of laughter, while he plotted his course, while he hesitated and cast around over the vast field of possible utterance, the jungle of expression in which he must presently select the one shape of words, the one image, it might be the one epithet that would suit him—while his eyes grew rounder and larger with their rolling twinkle as he foresaw his discovery and relished his approaching success: wait, wait! he seemed to say—you shall enjoy this with me in a moment—give me time! She waited, still precariously on the edge, all alert to receive it. Out it came, the period achieved, with a gathering momentum, and she snatched it away with her peal of mirth and carried it off on a further, wilder, airier flight. There was no hesitation in *her;* everything she possessed was at her finger's end, as quick as she needed it. She knew all that she thought, all that she remembered or fancied; she never had to look for the right thing, it was there; and her laugh, high and sharp, was cut short by the word that darted to meet the next challenge, the next absurdity—caught and returned in one movement. Here, in such talk, she let herself go;

here was freedom and breathable air and the joy of exercise; and her companions encouraged her—they admiringly, half-indulgently, entertained and courted her to her heart's content. It was more than a game of play, if you looked at them; it was like a sort of concerto, a concourse of instruments supporting the guest of honour. Henry James accompanied her with the whole weight of his orchestra. Howard Sturgis joined in with his nimble descant, so deceptively simple—joined in or dropped out as he chose; his way was always his own, whatever he did.

He did as he chose, and he gave the same liberty to everyone else. But Henry, great master of cases and situations, had other views, and his view of this visitor ascribed to her a position that she had to fill. She had placed herself in it or he placed her—anyhow he saw her there and commended her for it; his creation or hers, he approved it as good. He admired her effect in the world—he watched, he presided over it; he couldn't, if it really was her own doing, have designed or composed it for her more pictorially—it was as good as a fiction of his own. Here was America, brilliantly flashing upon Europe; here was fine old New York, secure and decent, the right tradition, the real thing; and here, upon that well-laid foundation, was her own skill, grace, intelligence, all of the best, flashing across to meet this Europe on the highest terms, any terms she pleased—she had only to make her own. Hither she came to take her place, with all that an old civilisation had to offer already hers, and with more into the bargain, a finer edge, a freer sweep—with a hand, in short, that he could trust, that he could count on to find and hold its own, never excessively or outlandishly, in the structure of the greatest world. If she was a novel of his own she did him credit; his eye could find no fault. All this was much more than her pretty little literary talent, the handful of clever little fictions of her own; but there was that too, *ce qui ne gâte rien,* and a distinguished little ornament of its kind, still further marking her for the discrimination of those who know. And then, beyond and beside it all, as he entertained her, as he created his talk for her with twitching mouth and roving eye, she was something quite different as well, and he loved her fondly. She had no fear of him, she didn't spoil or pet him with her homage. She was his equal friend, and the only woman of whom this could be said.

That was Henry; and Howard, if you looked to him, admired and loved her too, but with his own difference. He too plied her with his court, free-handed in his infinite variety. There was the swift dart of his wit, that looked so innocent; his demureness and sedateness, as it might be of a quiet old body in company too high and clever for him; and then his mockery and mimicry, his ribaldry, joyfully outrageous, blandly unblushing: there was no end to Howard, none to the riches of his comedy when he cared to scatter them. But there was always this about Howard's lavish effusion of himself upon his friends, that his eye upon you, when you caught it, fixed with a steadiness not to be deflected, seemed to leave you nothing, so to speak, but the clothes upon your back—not a thing that wasn't plainly and exclusively your own. Nothing else was expected of you, nothing else impressed him; the world and its opinion weighed upon him as a feather, blown aside unnoticed, save that he noticed everything. The angelic visitor, she knows so much, no doubt she knows this also—and yet I wonder does she know the whole of it? Henry stooped and gathered her into his imagination with an Olympian benediction; Howard laid his possessions as a tribute at her feet; but which of the two stood entirely independent to observe her, ringing her round with the lightness of his irony, so clear and light that it could be taken for simple air? She knew all about it, no doubt; everyone knew that it was no more possible to dazzle Howard than to exhaust his indulgence; and for her, as for all of us, his place in friendship was ever a little apart from the rest, in a corner of his own—where nothing mattered but what you really were, and that was what he loved. She laughed and chaffed with him, young and merry and confidential; they had their own understanding between them, and nothing else. That was Howard.

As for Henry, though he blessed her worldly adventures he couldn't stay to share them. For her the triumphs to which she was returning, which she would quickly be extending; they were very well for her and rightly hers. A greater lot was his—to be alone with his genius; for whatever his respect for the world, and indeed it brooked no question, it had never touched the sanctum where that communion reclaimed him—it dropped on the threshold of his work. He confided her, in departing, to Howard's inimitable care—turning, as I see him, with his foot on the carriage-step, to applaud their stars, to solemnize their conjunction—in short to deliver himself of a floral and ceremonial valediction for which the horses must stand and wait, till his great head dives and disappears into the vehicle with a trail of chuckles. He still remained with us when he was gone; we were never far from Henry James in those days and in that house at Windsor. He stayed while we talked of him—and what else could we talk of till this new addition to our stock of him, bequeathed by his latest visit, had been fixed in the form of art by Howard's matchless impersonation? Were Henry's tones and phrases more his own, more himself, when *he* uttered them, or when they were born again in Howard's reproduction of them? At any rate they lost nothing, so transmuted, and we kept them bright with use. How we lived on Henry in those days! The breadth of his humour, the swoop of his curiosity, the loftiness of his criticism, the dignity of his isolation—he was such a piece of work with all these that we could take him up and go on with him at any hour, for any time. He had just then finished the vast triple monument of his full-wrought art, the three big novels into which he withdrew for good and all from careless or casual frequentation; and the happy few who knew themselves earnest and attentive, tracking him up the winding stairs of his porcelain pagoda, were absorbed by the quest and its achievement. But the shining intruder, strange to say, by no means shared this diligence when it came to reading him. She glanced and passed, she whisked through him and out again—not empty-handed, naturally, but how much of that treasury is to be seized by glances? It was enough, I suppose, that she was herself a novel of his, no doubt in his earlier manner.

Moreover it was noticeable, when he departed and she remained behind, that life began to change—almost as though it were returning to its old condition in spite of her; things had ever an obstinate way of growing natural again where Howard was. She could now take a walk with him and his dogs in Windsor Park. That was briskly and gaily done, but soon done—and what then?

Time wore on; the lamps were brought in, tea was cleared away, Howard took up his knitting; and she sat by the fire, still very upright in her armchair, quick for talk, her eye ready for what should happen next—snapping perpetual cigarettes out of her little gold case, swiftly rustling across the room for a book and back to her chair, as taut and broad awake as though it weren't a comfortable evening by a glowing hearth, with the dogs now snoring in their baskets. Now was the time when she might turn her attention to the unobtrusive young man, believed literary in his aspirations, who was still there in the background; but she wasn't in the habit of delving into shyness, she was accustomed to see gifts laid before her, and this poor creature's gifts, if he had any, were seldom to hand at the right moment. And then the way of approach to her, the only apparent way, seemed still distressingly public—up a red carpet, so to speak, in a strong light, to a spot where you might, but after all might not, be pressed to take a seat beside her. The young man was interesting when you knew him—but would she see it? Yet she was a writer of books—books that I had finely read and acutely admired, books that I had even criticised in print; there was common ground between us if she chose to take it. But I had never seen a writer in our old world who kept such state as she did, and I couldn't go faltering up the royal carpet by my-self, with my awkward step. It *was* a little disappoint-ing—a little aggrieving too. But there it was; my place was in the shade.

Howard, raising his eyes from his knitting, took it all in, I fully knew with what amusement. Well, some of us have brains beyond our expertness, weight beyond our agility, and others, as this remarkable woman, have brains that fly to their fingers like an electric current, that dance in their feet like quicksilver. She couldn't be idle, and it was vain to think of detaining her if you hadn't the means to keep her occupied. She missed her work, she was itching to get back to it—her work that was creation of many kinds, in all sorts of material; and if she had such a bunch of talents in both hands, with all the freedom on earth to use them, no wonder that she couldn't bear to waste her time. Off with her, then, to the scene that she needs for her work—to the populous plastic world. It will always be amusing to watch her, as to watch any master of a craft who knows what he is about to a hair's breadth. Such an artist can't accept dictation from anyone, and you could bind the unicorn to harrow the valleys as soon as you could fasten this woman by any will that isn't hers. No matter for that: if she is all high-handed command she is all intelligence too, all fine discernment and generous enjoyment and large liberality. Were only the lords of creation all as freely to be trusted! It wasn't likely that *she* would overlook any stuff of good quality, were it the plainest, for ever; she wanted it all, she meant to have it and she would. But with the kingdoms of the earth lying open to view, sparkling under the sky, she couldn't have the patience to rake the grasses at her feet. In the course of time there might be a chance for all, even for those who are left behind. Let her go; some day one may overtake her.

II

New York and the Mount

It was once said of Edith Wharton, and she liked and repeated the remark, that she was a 'self-made man.' It was also said of her, and I dare say she would have accepted this too, but there would have been more to say about it, and we must be sure that we understand it aright—it was said of her that she was essentially the daughter of New York. I have no doubt that both these judgments, though they look contradictory, were true and just; and as for the second, which we must be careful about interpreting, I have luckily no call to explain what it meant or implied. I have only to point to the picture in which it is all set forth, the meaning of the phrase, the aspect of the place of her birth and nurture: to her own fiction, that is to say, or to the considerable part of it that paints the portrait of her own New York—very sharply to be distinguished, she would have us observe, from the New York of those who came after her, even by a short interval. Her New York, of seventy years since, has there the appearance of a well-rounded polity, as compact within its circuit as an old walled township, 'la cité antique,' before the days of spreading suburbs and liberties without the gates: such was the comfortable self-containment of its life and genius. New York, that now means indefinite mixture and towering height, then meant no great size and modest elevation, but within its bounds a society conscious of itself, aware of its order, sufficient for its needs, beyond any to be seen to-day, or perhaps in its own day either. It was in no way large enough to be unwieldy or out of hand. It had its choice traditions, not old enough to have loosened or diverged; its organised forms, too plain to be ignored; its customary law, too distinct and categorical to be evaded. I have heard that Edith's mother, a high authority on the subject, would count the names of all the families, in due order of degree, who composed the world to which her daughter was born; and there her world stopped short, it was implied, and no mistake about it. Edith Jones, in those young days, stood upon her own step, and a good one too, of a fine flight of stairs, declared the equal of any in the world, the '*scala nobile*' of the counted clans; she couldn't but know her place and be proud of it.

But she was a singular young woman. Though she was pleased with her place, well content to keep and adorn it, and never had the least inclination to flout the law under which she was born, she was determined to have a great deal more than the mere good portion prescribed for Edith Jones. Like a hungry young hawk, her mind was somehow to be fed; and she clutched at any sustenance within reach, wherever it appeared, tearing her way through it all with the passion to know, to see, to judge, which was her particular and private possession, never to be quenched or satisfied. An odd young thing, so rightly elegant, so acceptably attractive, so properly gay —and such a sharp beak of intelligence within, that pierced where it would, and that all the forms and laws of the world couldn't hold from its natural prey. Its prey

was distributed over a great field. Language and literature, art and history, all was one; she rifled the ages with
impartiality, and turned them, what is more, to her own
enduring account. There were books in her home, if none
too many; there was her kind proud father, admiring the
adventures of her curiosity if he didn't share them; and
there was also, by a piece of notable fortune, her good
German governess, friend of her youth and long after,
who shared and helped them out of her own sound store.
But mainly she supported herself, and she had a remarkably just instinct in her manner of setting to work.
Nothing was ever more unmistakable in Edith than the
quality of the foundations of her culture. She was never
delayed in trifling with the easy, the showy, the quickly
and the cheaply rewarding; she went straight for the best,
and no time lost; and she set up her standards once for all,
to serve her lifetime. She seemed to be excused the long
labour of trying the wrong turnings, following the wrong
leads, discarding misfits, such as most of us have to worry
through with patience; and this was fortunate, for she
had no patience at all or at any time for second thoughts
and anxious reviewals, only an eagerness, never exhausted, for further exploration and acquisition. Such
was the double life enjoyed by Miss Jones of New York,
the ornament of her circle. She was all that was right and
regular in her smooth clan-plumage, but the young hawk
looked out of her eyes.

Self-made, then, she certainly was in a manner of
speaking, and most efficiently made; but we can see that
she started with advantages. Of direct encouragement to
look and think for herself there may not have been much
to begin with, but in liberal opportunity to look far, to
find plenty to think about, her lot was favoured. If there

were not a great many ideas around her, there was one
that flourished abundantly under her parents' roof, and
for her it was the most important of all—it was the idea
of Europe. Well-furnished New York, with everything
handsome about it, was sufficient for itself, no doubt, but
it was far from disowning its heritage of Europe. The new
world, pleasing itself, had taken a different way from the
old; but old and new had been one world before they
parted, and their common past belonged equally to both.
New York held its share in Europe, very properly, as its
own by right of inheritance; and young Edith and her
parents not only spoke and thought and felt in the idiom
that had descended to them, they also returned to their
past in long and leisurely European sojourns—one of
years when she was a child, another when she was a girl.
In France, in Italy and Spain, she had innocently played
and earnestly studied long before she entered into her
later possession of their freedom. It is true, or so I have
understood, that some ancient tale of family dissension
still kept America a little cool and reserved in English
air—as though it 'risked its dignity' (I am quoting an
American novelist, the one we are watching) when it
exposed itself to the glances, possibly tactless, of cousinly
eyes. Even Mrs. Jones, I heard her daughter say, found
herself a trifle cramped and beset, on our side of the sea,
by old New York's respectable fear of appearing to 'run
after' a society suspected, perhaps with reason, of not
always clearly apprehending the distinction between the
right New York and the wrong. These are delicate
matters; but it is plain at any rate that France was the
favourite for long visits, France where there had never
been any unpleasantness in the past—quite the reverse.
And this little party, parents and daughter, had its own

reason, a simpler one, for preferring genial to uncertain climates; for Edith was still a young girl when her good father's health gave way and declined, quietly and sadly, to his death at Cannes. She had always been in effect an only child, her two brothers being grown young men from her earliest memory. Now she was alone with her mother, and New York reclaimed her.

There, no doubt, was her place at that time and for a long while to come—there or wherever else (it happened at first to be chiefly Newport) her own New York was about her. When she was married, as she very soon was, she still remained in her place, securely fixed in it, highly concious of it. Her marriage indeed opened the way, as much as she pleased, to easy travel, and now there were constant and regular flights to Europe, including one, ever memorable, that raked the Mediterranean as far as the isles of Greece; she was a passionate traveller, never so happy as when she took the road to see the world. But still she returned to her place at the journey's end; she helped herself in her wanderings to what she needed, a magnificent lapful, and carried it home. It was not for her to be hungering in her native air for things that it didn't provide; of these she could always bring back store in plenty, with vision and memory refreshed and enriched—enough to last till next time and the next. It was no question with her as it was with some, of an air in which she couldn't thrive, a life in which she couldn't accomplish her purpose. She was never one to linger helpless and undecided in conditions that didn't suit her; where she was, there was Edith Wharton on her ground, and she wouldn't have been there if the ground were insufficient for her needs. Was there a touch of defiance, I might ask, in her attitude of assurance?—as though it were not for us to question the quality and suitability of anything that was good enough for *her*. Something of this sort may perhaps be divined beneath the surface, always shining, not always softly or mildly glowing, that she presented to the world. It would be harder to say of her than of most people that there were wants unmet, questions unanswered within—supposing there were. But at least she now, and for many years yet, was at home in her own land, in the life she led and the houses she created, with her good-natured and admiring husband; and in this phase of her progress we shall now, thanks to an old and valued friend of those days, take a long direct look at her, where she holds her ground and her position with clear effect. Mr. Daniel Berkeley Updike, founder of the Merrymount Press at Boston, was well placed for a friendly and intimate view of them both, Edith and her husband, for many of their American years; and now let us look.

My first meeting with Mrs. Wharton [writes Mr. Updike] was at Newport about 1897, where, when stopping with Mr. Ogden Codman, I was asked to lunch at Pen Craig Cottage, a small house with a garden, facing Pen Craig, formerly the Jones place, where Mrs. Wharton had passed her child-hood. Pen Craig Cottage was a delightful little house, charmingly appointed and arranged with that taste and fine sense of scale that distinguished the interior of the three or four houses which she lived in before her departure for France. Later on this house was given up, and a larger one, formerly belonging to the Henry Crams, was bought. This place, called Land's End, was at the lower end of the cliff walk, where the waves beat ceaselessly upon the ledges bordering the grounds. A less intimate and more ambitious house than the cottage, it never seemed to me so interesting, but it was managed with the same civilised attention to comfort and detail that made the cottage so agreeable an interior. There was a good deal of entertaining there; yet I never felt that Edith cared much for Land's End, possibly because rocks and breaking seas and far horizons were too elemental a setting for the elegance she liked. After some years, tiring of Newport, land was bought near Lenox, in the hills of western Massachusetts, and a house built there after plans for which she was largely responsible. It was charmingly placed on a slight knoll and was christened The Mount, not because it was one, but because some old family place had been so named.

Lenox was far more successful than Newport for long seasons away from town, though rather limited as to any large number of congenial people; and neighbouring ladies were sometimes made uncomfortable by the suspicion—by no means unfounded—that Mrs. Wharton was ironically amusing at their expense. I remember one evening in particular when she returned from a dinner remarking, 'The XYZ's have decided, they tell me, to have books in the library.' These sayings were repeated, generally inaccurately, and did not increase her popularity. I recall, too, once going of an afternoon to see an old lady with several unmarried daughters at a moment when one of Mrs. Wharton's earlier books had been published. One of the younger ladies thought it sad, another morbid, a third unpleasant. Mrs. Wharton replied, cleverly but with some impatience, to these charges, and the mother, seeing her elderly brood routed by these rejoinders, said in a majestic tone, 'In short, Mrs. Wharton, as a family we demand cheer!' I don't know why I was dragged along to pay this visit on a hot summer's day, but as we left the house Edith whispered, 'I think they thought it was a visit of Isabella d'Este and Aldus Manutius.'

There were, however, a few people in Lenox who were sympathetic and interesting. And of these the Crams, who lived at Highwood after leaving Newport, were Edith's most intimate friends. Ethel Cram was perhaps the person who had most influence with her of any woman at that period, for she had intellectual capacities that Edith respected, and clear and unswerving views which gave her certainty on matters about which Edith was not so sure. I have always felt that the stodginess of most of Mrs. Wharton's 'good' people in her books came from being over-dosed with the talk of ladies whose doubts about the Lenox rector's orthodoxy seemed to her of very slight importance. To Ethel Cram, who was a woman of the world without being a worldly woman, Edith listened; and had she lived, perhaps Edith's life in certain respects might have been different.

When we first met, Mrs. Wharton was working in collaboration with Ogden Codman on *The Decoration of Houses*—for the title-page and binding of which I was responsible. It was an able book and still holds its own—though at the time of its publication some fun was poked at the childless authors about their chapter on nurseries. Always intellectually alert as she was, and with a cultivated approach to art and letters, I am not sure that litera- ture and the desire to write played so large a part in her life in these early days as one might·suppose in reading *A Backward Glance*. Both she and her husband loved simple yet luxurious living, knew how to effect this intelligently, and were past mas- ters in the art of entertaining; and in this there was between them a complete unanimity of taste. In other words, at that period they were fashionable people—if one still uses that Victorian word—and I do not think that there was any great longing on Edith's part that this should be otherwise.

I do not remember any house where the hos- pitality was greater or more full of charm than at The Mount. As one thinks of it in retrospect the word 'civilised' comes to one's mind. The garden was a great interest to Edith, and the opening of vistas and planting of trees was a constant amuse- ment to Teddy, and they both shared in the love of dogs and horses. Edith was very learned about gardens, and she and a neighbour, Miss Charlotte Barnes, used to hold interminable, and to me rather boring, conversations about the relative merits of various English seedsmen and the precise shades of blue or red or yellow flowers that they could guaran- tee their customers. I have never thought it very in- teresting to hear about other people's gardens, and have laughed at the prosy discourses of their own- ers until I had one of my own, when I found myself victimizing guests in precisely the same way. Edith

was conscious of my half-hearted interest in horti-
culture, and on one particularly dull autumn afternoon when she was directing some planting, I
asked her if there was not something I could do—
hoping that there wasn't! With a malicious glint in
her eye she replied, 'Yes, you can pick off the
withered petunias that border the fountain.' If you
have ever tried that particular task you will realise
the punishment inflicted.

The three principal rooms at The Mount were
a library, a drawing-room and a dining-room. The
dining-room had French windows which opened
on a broad terrace overlooking the formal parterres
of the garden, and this terrace was shaded by an
immense striped awning. Beyond that, a lawn
sloped to a meadow stretching to the border of a
little wooded lake. One day when a party for lunch
had gathered on the terrace, Mr. Choate arrived,
accompanied by the Austrian Ambassador. 'Ah,
Mrs. Wharton,' he said as he stepped from the
house, 'when I look about me I don't know if I am
in England or in Italy.'

And what an amusing and delightful house it
was to stay in—not a bit sophisticated in its atmosphere—full of gaiety and fun of a very simple
sort: we laughed until we cried! Both Edith and
Teddy loved to entertain amusing people, though
sometimes I thought them more amusing than well-
bred. On that point Teddy was more sensitive than
Edith, who could occasionally tolerate men who
interested her when he could not; for without being an intellectual man, he had, besides warm-
heartedness and charm, that intuitive good breed-

ing which detects at a glance pretentiousness and sham. No hosts were more considerate of their guests; and there was real consideration too for the servants and those employed on the place. These were the days of horses and an occasional motor, in which perilous and halting excursions were made to Ashfield to see the Norton family and to other not very distant points, which then seemed very distant indeed. But neither when they were alone nor when there were visitors at The Mount was any servant required to do more than necessary duty on Sundays or holidays. I once said to Edith, 'You are the most considerate person to your servants I ever saw.' She replied rather seriously, 'Perhaps that is because I was brought up in a household where there was no consideration for them at all.' Kindness and helpfulness to those less fortunately placed than themselves were traits that both Edith and Teddy shared equally, and I remember with what mischievous amusement they confounded some snobbish acquaintance by marked attention to their children's somewhat downtrodden governess.

They were, however, dangerous adversaries if liberties were taken in giving advice as to behaviour. Teddy had a ready wit—as may be gathered from his clever retort to George Moore recorded in *A Backward Glance*—and one day, being late for a luncheon engagement in Newport, rather than keep his host waiting he hailed a passing butcher's cart and rode up Bellevue Avenue in it. A day or two later an acquaintance (newly 'arrived' in Newport in more senses than one), meeting Teddy, said, 'Wharton, I hear that you rode up the Avenue in a butcher's cart. I wouldn't do that if I were you.' 'No,' said Teddy, 'if I were you I wouldn't do that either.'

By this time her first volume of short stories had appeared—and she was so pleased and surprised, and Teddy so proud of her cleverness and success. When *The Greater Inclination* was published by Scribner's she stipulated with them that I must be employed to print it. To her thoughtful act the Merrymount Press owed not merely the prestige of printing her books, but also the printing of many other volumes for Scribner's—indeed we were constantly employed by the firm until it set up a press of its own. Nothing could have helped me more, just then, than the Scribner connection, for it showed the Press could hold its own with larger printing-houses; and this was all due to Edith, who used her influence as generously, intelligently and effectively then, as she did many times before and since, for persons or causes that she thought deserved a 'lift.'

At Lenox her writing was done early in the day, though very little allusion was made to it, and none at all to the infinite pains that she put into her work or her inexhaustible patience in searching for the material necessary to perfect it. By eleven o'clock she was ready for friends and engagements, for walking or garden-work. One windy autumn afternoon we were driving in the country near Lenox, and on the top of a hill on the left of the road stood a battered two-story house, unpainted, with a neglected door-yard tenanted by hens and chickens, and a few bedraggled children sitting on the stone steps before the open door. 'It is about a place like that,' said Mrs. Wharton, 'that I mean to write a story. Only last week I went to the village meeting-house in Lenox and sat there for an hour alone, trying to think what such lives would be, and some day I shall write a story about it.' And I suppose the result was shown in the writing of *Ethan Frome.* I have sometimes felt that Mrs. Wharton, in her less successful books, solved problems of the heart with the head; and those situations which passion or feeling could successfully disentangle were somewhat lamely met by behaviour based on an intellectual process. But in her best pages, and notably in *Ethan Frome,* she struck a far deeper note.

No one was more quick-witted than Edith, nor more intolerant of pretentiousness. She happened to be stopping in Boston just at the moment when Mrs. Gardner was arranging the interior of Fenway Court. Mrs. Gardner loved to veil her proceedings with an air of mystery, and she permitted people to have a peep at her house, admitted by a 'postern' (which was merely a side-door) at some precise and generally rather inconvenient moment. If this appointment was not exactly met, the 'postern' was closed and the unfortunate late-comer left without. I think Mrs. Gardner rather enjoyed these early morning appointments, and perhaps also the failure of tardy guests to enjoy her hospitality. Knowing that Mrs. Wharton was in town, she sent word to her that if she wished to see the house and would arrive promptly at twelve minutes past eight in the morning, Mrs. Gardner would consent to show it to her. Mrs. Wharton replied that she was never up at that hour, and the invitation was declined. Some friends of ours possessed an enormous country-house, so vast and magnificent as to be quite uncomfortable. Edith and I happened to be paying a visit there at the same time. 'This house,' she said, 'has all the inconveniences of an hotel without any opportunity to complain at the office.' To a rather impertinent Frenchman who asked to see The Mount and who said somewhat patronizingly as he departed that he approved of it all except a bas-relief in the entrance-hall, she replied, 'I assure you that you will never see it here again.'[*]

When Mr. Updike first met her, in 1897, she was thirty-five, and she had been living as he saw her for fifteen years (she was married in 1882)—and only then, at that age, was she so much as beginning to think about writing a book, and that only a book of advice on the adornment of houses. What *had* she been doing in all that time? Mr. Updike has given us the singular answer: she had been leading a 'fashionable' life—I thank him for not shirking the word; and if the word is allowed the proper amplitude of its day it is not to be questioned. It is a fact that she reached the half-way of life without discovering or divining that she was a writer of books; we have her own testimony too in this matter—she gives it in *A Backward Glance*, and seems to think it no great wonder. But what! For observe that this was not a case of one who was hesitating, holding back, shyly or mis-

[*] Mr. Updike kindly wrote and sent me the foregoing pages in 1938. He died in 1941.

trustfully refraining from an ambition and a dream of the future; there was not even the dream. True enough she had scribbled copiously as a girl, like any other clever girl; but like any other sensible woman (as if she were that!) she had put away her novels and poems for good when she stepped into her own real life; and in the light of what her own real life was to be, when at last she reached it, the case is surely one of the strangest we have known. It is easy to say that her gift of creation had always been used, for she had the life that was under her hand to shape and embellish to the top of its form; and this she did from the first, as we see, with an art that impressed all beholders. And yet when I think of her in those long early years and fail to see her, as all through the long later years she was always to be seen, with her mind possessed of the book she was writing, her eye darting off to the book she would write—I feel that nothing is really said by such suggestions. But there it is: she lighted on her vocation in course of time as a man might discover in himself, unsuspected before, an aptitude for a game of skill. It hadn't occurred to him before to handle a cue, and it didn't dawn upon Edith Wharton till the middle of her life that she was a writer born. Well, she dressed, she furnished her house, she fed her guests, she laid out her garden, all better than anyone else. I never heard of such an apprenticeship for a writer, but it served in this case.

Things were very different, of course, by the time she was creating The Mount; the discovery had been made, and she knew herself once for all. The change in her state must have its own chapter; but if it really began, and we must believe that it did, with the fancy of teaching others to have houses as beautifully trimmed as her own, it is but just to look for a moment at the talent that worked so much more good than it intended. Not that I undertake to estimate her art in this matter; I only know that there was a great deal of it, and that it produced house after house in the course of years, and each one recalled by all who saw it as an exquisite creation. Too exquisite, said some, perfect to the point of 'coldness,' if warmth requires any trifle of disorder or inconsistency, any allowance for a change of mood from the highest to the not so high; the eye might hunger, perhaps, for just one object out of place, and not the best of its kind. But I have noticed that we all have a clear conviction of the degree to which art should be mixed with chance to be convenient in the home, and it is the mixture to which we happen to be used; and anyhow nobody could deny that to be a guest in a house of Mrs. Wharton's was a deeply, deliciously, delicately luxurious experience. And by the way, if it is held that for a house to be humanly habitable there must be other animals in it of some sort, there was always a dog or two about Edith in her home, a small dog of the yapping kind, a still smaller of the fidgeting and whining breed—dogs that had to be called, caressed, rebuked—dogs that had to be led out or carried in or taken for a run. She was one of those passionate lovers of animals who dislike all animals but dogs; I suppose she would have excepted horses, but of horses she was secretly afraid—I have her word for it. As for children—but at this point I will only say that in those days I don't think children were missed. She had announced, at the age of eight, that she intended to have no children till she was sixty, and then a nice little family at leisure—'an excellent plan, I still think,' I remember her saying. But of children on another occasion. Here meanwhile is a vivid note, from her friend Mrs. Gordon Bell, that is now to the point.

We first knew Mrs. Wharton in 1906, through a common interest in the Society for the Prevention of Cruelty to Animals. We, with a few other people, had become dissatisfied with its work, which seemed careless, haphazard, and open to suspicion of graft. Edith Wharton joined the insurgent group, and many times we met in her house near 79th Street on Park Avenue, one of the first little brownstone twin houses converted into one and considered very far 'up town.' Her vivid interest and keen mind, though sometimes ignoring the legal aspects of the case, went far to defeat obstruction, and her many and well-known friends helped very much to swell the ranks of the members. That was the beginning of a long and much-treasured friendship, and perhaps no better foundation for such a friendship could be found than sympathetic indignation and hard work to right a wrong done to the helpless.

We stayed with her that summer at Lenox, and I think every summer after that until she settled in Paris. The Mount was a different sort of revelation of herself. Here was Edith Wharton the artist, content with nothing less than the best in the gardening, the cooking, the furnishing and housekeeping of her place. Everything in it was harmonious, brought to the same degree of perfection by minute care combined with faultless taste. The hard-working writer, the traveller, the woman of letters, seemed merged into the hostess. The first time she showed me my room I remember saying to her, 'What a perfect desk—everything conceivably needed for writing is there'; and I can see her little deprecating smile as she answered, 'Oh, I am rather a housekeeperish person.' The same diversity appeared in her conversation; when her guests were literary or very intelligent, her brilliant mind and extraordinary memory shone like a sparkling diamond; and even with people who merely amused her, she could sit for hours over the fire or out on the terrace and tell or hear stories, funny incidents, anything that struck her sense of humour; she could laugh over them like a child—a somewhat caustic child perhaps. It was much harder to get her to talk about her own books; except to a very small inner circle she never spoke of them of her own accord, and always seemed to be on her guard if others mentioned them to her. Being a very normal person she preferred men to women, and often terrified the latter with a cold stare; but she was frequently quite unconscious of it, except when they were gushing—*that* she couldn't stand. I remember once, when I first knew her, looking up and finding her staring at me with what seemed an unfriendly gaze. I said, 'What have I done to be looked at so disapprovingly?'—and she said, 'Oh no, I was just thinking that I liked your hat.' But many women who only knew her slightly have said to me, 'She looks at me as if I were a worm.' Was it an inherited manner or was it self-defence?

Which indeed?—or was it possibly something else, or even many other things? It is clear already that it will be vain, in the company of those who knew Edith Wharton, to pretend that she was always sweetly and mercifully kind; we shall too often catch one another's eye over our memories of her at moments when she was nothing of the sort. But this, I believe, will also be noticeable—that we shall constantly disagree in our condoning or extenuating explanations of the sharp points in her behaviour; sufficient reasons for these we shall have to find, in a woman of her large charity, but we shall argue about them to the end. For my part I prefer to wait for other suggestions, of which there will be no lack, before offering a word on the subject, only admitting at once that nobody can rightly picture her as she was who does not see her capable at times of marked—and often apparently quite uncalled-for—asperity. She was one of the few people I have ever known who did what severe ladies used to do so readily in novels: she 'drew herself up'—there were occasions when her action and attitude could only be thus described—and wasn't at all disturbed by the embarrassment or confusion she created. I must own that I can't agree with Mrs. Bell (what did I say?) that she was ever unconscious of her effect; I think she always knew her intention very well, and her stare didn't often mean only that she was admiring a hat. Perhaps the neatly rounded world in which she was bred was not very good for her in this respect. It was small—and she couldn't be unaware that she was the cleverest person in it; it was small—and so it was quite clear who were outside it, and they could be kept outside; it was small—and it might *look* small in comparison with other worlds, if its worth weren't unmistakably asserted by its bearing. And here I am exploring and suggesting after all, but in doing so I have led up to another little picture under my hand, which shall close this chapter. There was a young Englishwoman, newly married and established in New York, in the heart of the citadel, when Mrs. Wharton was in the first of her celebrity as an author of books; and the picture of their meeting is now re-called after many years.

It was with excitement, not unmingled with apprehension, that one afternoon during my first winter in America I approached Edith Wharton's door in Park Avenue. She was the person I most wished to meet in New York, for the two volumes of her stories that I had read had aroused my warmest admiration. I knew her to be clever, and I had heard that she could be formidable; but she was a friend of my husband's family and I had been invited to pay her a call.

At first sight the house was reassuring. It was small, plain and unpretentious, and might have stood unnoticed in a quiet corner of Brompton. Once inside I was not so sure. It was English cer-tainly, but with a minute and studied perfection quite unknown to me in English houses of its kind. The drawing-room too, where I had vaguely hoped to find Mrs. Wharton seated at her literary labours, was as barren of any sign of habitual occupation as all the other New York drawing-rooms in which I had waited for an intimidating interval before my hostess rustled in. When Mrs. Wharton did ap-pear, she, like all the other ladies I had called on, had evidently changed into an afternoon dress— brown silk it was, of a shade admirably suiting her

bright brown hair and eyes, and alarmingly neat
in every detail. I suppose I had not actually expected disordered hair and inky fingers—her writing certainly did not suggest any disarray in the
writer; but I had perhaps imagined that she would
look less like the other New York ladies of fashion
than she did. Nevertheless I tried after a while to
offer her my shy tribute to her work; but she
brushed it aside with a light but final 'Ah, your
husband must have given you my little tales'—and
proceeded to enquire about the mutual friends she
was sure we must have in London. 'Dear Mrs.
White,' she said, 'did you see her before you sailed?'
I truthfully replied that I had, and did not feel
bound to add that it was the first time I ever *had*
seen her, and that on my husband's presentation of
me I had received the immediate impression that
she preferred her clever young men unattached.
'And Howard Sturgis—did you go to see him at
Windsor?' I had not, and could only say that I
believed he was at our wedding, and that his
brother Harry was a friend of my father's. She dismissed his brother Harry and passed on to Henry
James. Him I had met at a dinner-party, but owing
to my youth and unimportance had never come
within speaking distance of the great man. A pause
ensued. London rather unexpectedly appeared to
me as distinguished only by the presence of these
brilliant American conversationalists, and I seemed
to have nothing to say about any of them. I plunged
boldly and wildly. 'You see,' I said, 'I went chiefly
to balls and big parties, with my parents, like those
at the Foreign Office.' 'Ah yes,' she said, 'those Lon-

don crowds—one can't get much out of *them.*' Suddenly a picture arose in my mind of a great staircase, at the head of which stood a gracious lady arrayed with every advantage of jewelled attire; beside her a slight small man, almost completely covered with the ribbons and insignia of his many decorations; each of them in converse with a royal personage. Around and beside me on the stairs thronged cabinet ministers, diplomats, judges, field-marshals, men of distinction in every branch of life, and with them their ladies, properly adorned for the great occasion. Was there indeed nothing to be got out of all that? Not much talk certainly, that was true enough—but still!—At this moment to my relief a man entered the room. 'Oh Edith,' he said, 'I think I've worked out quite a good plan for those rooms.' 'Mr. Codman'—she turned to me half in explanation, half in introduction—'is kindly helping me with some plans.' But I was already on my feet, glad of the excuse. Mr. Codman politely accompanied me to the front-door, and while I was struggling with my unfamiliar over-shoes, for there was snow on the ground, Mrs. Wharton leant over the banisters, thinking I had already gone, and called to him in a warm, kind, eager voice that I had not yet heard: 'What do you think, Ogden—could one in a little house like this allow a Chippendale clock in the hall?' I liked that voice—though the importance attached to the tiny problem seemed excessive in one who had lightly waved aside so much of London. As I walked home up Park Avenue I reflected that though I had called on another

[32]

New York lady I had not yet met Edith Wharton.

Our next meeting was far more fortunate—but of that I must be given the chance to speak later on.

III

A writer of books

It was Edith Wharton, however, who might have been seen in her house in New York,* on a certain day a few years before, tearing up and down the stairs like a creature possessed, mad with excitement. On that day a real editor of a magazine, a very fine one too, had written to say that he accepted and would publish a piece of her writing that she had sent him—it happened to be a small pair of poems; and it is surely a pleasing sight to behold this lofty and elegant lady running wild in the joy of her promotion. 'Is it really *me?*' she said to herself, as we can all tenderly remember saying once: 'am I too an author?' It was as fresh and sweet to her as to the hungriest young beginner to whom fame has beckoned from a printed page, his own, his first. She recognised her calling on the spot. Mrs. Wharton, then, is a writer, and very soon real writers are telling her so and regarding her as one of themselves. Who would have thought it? Her family, her friends of the clans of New York, might be slower to understand that she was henceforth a new woman; and indeed, as we have seen for ourselves, she scarcely encouraged them to do so—enough for them that she was Mrs. Wharton of New

* An earlier one, in Madison Avenue.

York in her drawing-room. But there were others who knew and were permitted to know better; and she set to her work, guarding a place for her work in her decorate existence—not only never betraying a ruffled hair or an inky finger, but always conducting her life in the world, as a full-rigged ship under sail, with an eye for every detail and time for every claim. How she managed it all was a wonder, at least to those who have the power, which she never had, of leaving a minute of the day to look after itself, in idle vacancy. There was no slack moment allowed in any calendar of hers; each had to be always at attention where she commanded.

What was more surprising, after the long years she had passed without a pen in her hand, was the entirely serious and professional spirit in which she now took it up. I am not saying, of course, that she stepped at once into full possession of her talent and the knowledge of its use; she had far to go for that. But just as she seemed never to have tripped or fumbled in anything else she had set herself to do, so she now proceeded to handle this new matter boldly and exactly, with no confused or wavering touch. Her action had all the marks of a writer whose work is his life, none of the amateur who finds time in life for a by-play. One sign in particular I note—or rather it is noted for me by a friend who watched her in those days, a friend herself bred in the purest air of literary integrity; it was her 'fine indifference to praise—her frank and easy attitude to the reputation she was beginning to make.' This, though it may sound a little nobler than the real meaning within it—for, as a poet once remarked, praise, so long as it is copious and unqualified, is sweet to every master-mind, sweet but *irrelevant*—is very rightly said of Edith Whar-

ton, and there could be no clearer signal of work pro-
gressing on lines well laid. When once she was started in
earnest her ways with her work, her manner toward it,
were always perfect. The hapless novice, fondling and
cajoling his offspring—anything to induce it to brighten
up and look more assured!—was never Edith. She was
neither shy of her work nor in love with it; she looked it in
the face, and would have no whims or airs. She respected,
she believed in it, and needed none to persuade her that
she might. Certainly she had a dread, not unwholesome,
of appearing in her world as a social muse, admired as a
curiosity among her kind; and this reluctance, I dare
say, she might push to an extreme that was ungracious.
But with those to whom she did open the history of her
ever-active art she was frank and free in all simplicity,
always ready to show and consider her hand, to listen
and learn. The time was to come when she had so controlled her craft that it had little history to relate, indeed
perhaps too little. But in these early years she was for
ever working her way forward step by step, cautious and
clear-sighted, mastering each and advancing to the next.
It was the manner and movement—quite apart from
actual achievement, which I don't discuss—of a master.

Here once more was her inborn gift, her native
efficiency that stuck to her in every field she essayed.
She required no example to instruct her in a business-
like attack. The few clever critical people who made the
inner circle that she drew round her—tightly and
closely, and by this time more and more so—could never
have taught her, had she needed it, to break her new
ground with such decision; and as for the society of the
profession in general where her work belonged, it was
never, oddly enough, to know her familiarly or retain

her long. She neither endured nor understood the tone, the preoccupation, the custom of thought, which prevail in places and companies where working days are a matter of course, and their decoration an incident. I should have supposed that there was no influence more fatal to an adventurous talent than that of a small band of the elect in a resolutely social world; everything in such a case should make for choiceness in miniature, for a fanciful refinement, for a few tenuous graces in a garden enclosed. But it had no such effect upon Edith Wharton; it was precisely that strain of exhausted dilettantism that always had her scorn. And so it is strange to me how she can have failed to gravitate, in spite of herself, towards anyone within reach, however plainly outside the garden, who was vigorously working and passionately talking in a broader style. That, however, meant Boston, and in Boston, I discern, her glittering plumage appeared misplaced; she was under suspicion there—not justly, but I am sure she did little to dispel it. The fact is that she was not enticed by any school of discourse or enquiry that cleaved to America as its home, or by any commotion of the mind that was loudly native in its zeal; she had no mission to America for her part. In short the story of her intellectual adventures, as told by herself, contains no mention of the name of William James.

But one household there was of academic consecration, and in very Boston too, where she made a friend who could give her more authoritative help, more instructed sympathy than she had yet enjoyed. She did not fail to find in Charles Eliot Norton, what so many had found before her, an influence discerning and humane. His was the house in those days where the banner of tradition was upheld with unshaken fidelity.

Piously, without noise or heat, great memories were served and honoured in that domain; and if it too in its way was a charmed enclosure, it was one that was open to the wide mild heaven of the past, in the serene of a long day filled with untiring study and illustrious company. Here indeed was a salutary atmosphere for anyone with whom the world was much—here where so many great spirit-voices still reverberated in tranquillity, holding and sharpening the attentive ear. Edith Wharton was gratefully indebted to this friend, and as for him it must have been pleasing to meet her eager and accurate pounce upon the value of his friendship. He recognised the quality of her power, and welcomed her to the freedom of his books and studies whenever she appeared. His summer retreat was happily within reach of The Mount, and thither she often made her way, returning with many spoils. He was indeed the one person to whom she *went*—whom she sought out on ground that was not her own, for she could arrive at him in no other way. There were not many in her life to whom she ever thus resorted. Norton was the first and in her American days the only one; and his share in her schooling was to show her the picture of a life singly dedicated to a high service. And now his daughter, only survivor of that household, will speak further of all this, in words and accents that recall those days as no one else could now evoke them.

It is difficult [writes Miss Elizabeth Norton] to look back and trace the origins of such friendships, for founded on sympathetic intellectual interests they are of the essence of timelessness. The Whartons and Nortons were of that same Boston group, very small in earlier days, which grew up in friendly intimacy; but Teddy's New York wife came from a more or less alien society to these somewhat rigid and austere New Englanders. One knew of his marriage—that was about all; for they lived in New York or Newport, the Newport that was fast changing from the days when it was the summer-home of delightful Southerners who made close friendships with the Nortons (who lived there then also)—to be bitterly broken by the Civil War. Unconsciously to us all, life began to change from simplicity to vulgarity somewhere in the late eighties, and about then also one began to realise that the society which seemed so aimless held voices unknown. It was my sister Sara who recognised Edith Wharton's genius in some verses printed in *Scribner's* or *Harper's*. Not long after they met in the house of mutual friends in New York. You would have said there was not much chance of sympathy: Edith, then shy, outwardly worldly, and measuring life, and living, by worldly standards—and those New York standards; and Sally, as she was known to all, so obviously different—brought up in the sheltered cloisters of Shady Hill, her grandparents' and father's home, influenced mainly by intellectual and spiritual rather than social values, but with that subtle gift of lovely looks and charm which beguiled all and quickly won the affection and interest of the more sophisticated yet brilliant Edith.

When Edith first came to Shady Hill I do not remember, and I do not think her visits there were many—Boston did not see her often. In those days society occupied her and Teddy, and her interests then were many, but always intellectualised. For years she was absorbed in the study of houses, furniture, and of course gardens; she had a flair for creation, but once the house in hand was finished her interest ceased and she must create anew. So it was that Newport lost interest, and she moved to Lenox, the New England village, once the home of Fanny Kemble and Catherine Sedgwick, soon to become the Newport of the Berkshire hills. There once more she created afresh, and it was during these years we saw most of her. Life in Lenox was the same social routine as in Newport. She had little in common with the summer colony and they did not find her very sympathetic; her natural shyness unconsciously impressed her intellectual superiority upon people, and she lived remotely. Her house, her garden, her appointments were all perfect—money, taste and instinct saw to every detail; yet the sense of a *home* was not there, and I think that perhaps is a quality one always missed in her surroundings, and perhaps it was a quality she realised in both Shady Hill and Ashfield. Her houses were all perfect, but cold; there was never the sound of young and ardent feet, of romping dogs (though dogs she always had and *loved*, but they were Papillons or Pekinese), of music, of games.

I do not think she was ever young in the sense that we were, for it was the fire of her brain in those days that made life such a thrill to her, while we were nothing more than young eager hearts. Lenox and Ashfield were about forty miles apart, and the drive along the Berkshire trail, through typical New England villages, gave her the setting and the idea for *Ethan Frome*, her classic. A lovely drive it was across the hills well watered by brooks and rivers. It meant, of course, taking time and spending at least one night, sometimes more, and we all looked forward to every such visit.

Life at Ashfield was as informal as it was the reverse at Lenox; there were no neighbours to call in for a dinner-party, but the Whartons came really for endless talk. My father's library was small at Ashfield compared to that at Shady Hill; but even so I think Edith never went away without borrowing some book or having her intellectual horizon widened by my father's sympathy and very real admiration for her great gifts. Many years later she wrote (1926): 'Thank you so much for copying that passage from your father's letter. It touches me very much to find that he believed in me all those long years ago, and when I think what it would have meant to know *then*, when all my dreams were still in my head, and I never hoped to be able to express them, I am saddened by the endless waste of sympathy and opportunity.'

She was not much of a walker, but she followed my father to High Pasture, a hill he owned and was very fond of, saw the beauty of it, expressed in later years by a sonnet he cared for. She was at her best at such times, and those who knew her at Lenox would hardly have recognised her at Ashfield, where, no longer shy, she expanded and expressed herself easily. Later on the visits came oftener, but were shorter, as with motors it was easy to come to lunch and return for dinner, and my father's strength did not allow for more.

From Windsor, July 7, 1909, Edith wrote to my sister: 'I always evoke your dear father in his library at Ashfield, or in the basket chair outside, under the trees . . . Do you remember the day we sat on the verandah and your father read Donne to us? And that evening, in the sitting-room, he read Matthew Arnold. I think it was once when Walter Berry was with me, and I have always kept a specially charming memory of that afternoon and evening. But best of all I like to picture him as I saw him that last time at Shady Hill, last summer, coming so gallantly down the steps to tell Cook what road to take to go to Beverly. It was such a pleasant last vision of him, in full alertness and activity.'

There are several points in Miss Norton's pleasant memories that I should like to take up. (The reader will have observed that another explanation of Mrs. Wharton's chillier regards has duly appeared, her shyness: I make a note of that!) But the name of Walter Berry, here first heard, must be attended to without further delay; for already it had long played (indeed from before her marriage) too important a part in the progress we are watching to be overlooked or put aside. To this friend of her life she has paid her own tribute in some deeply charged pages of A Backward Glance, charged with much more than they say, and it would be easy to leave the subject in her hands. She undoubtedly felt that it was to him she owed, as to no one else, the stirring of her imagination, the training of her thought, the knowledge and development of her talent, and that the wisdom of his counsel, accompanying her to the day of

his death, was the support of her career. It is as it may
be. But it happens to me again as it has happened before: with so many of her friends about me I am not
to evade their expressive looks; for they all have their
opinion of the manner in which this man affected
Edith's story, and I conceive that in this case their
opinion is one and the same. None of her friends, to put
it plainly, thought she was the better for the surrender
of her fine free spirit to the control of a man, I am ready
to believe, of strong intelligence and ability—but also,
I certainly know, of a dry and narrow and supercilious
temper. Neither he indeed nor anyone else could chill
the wide warmth of her response to all beauty, and no
one, it is very sure, taught her to write but herself with
her assiduous practice; but as for the ideas, the intellectual fare on which she was to live for so long, his influence was evident, and I call it (I seem to meet many
an assenting eye) disastrous. The education that she
took from him was long to hold her fast, and I believe
that whenever she seemed (as there were times when
she did) to shut up her mind in a box, and so much for
that, the reason went back to Walter Berry. Anyhow
there he was, an inevitable factor in her circle—*he* was
not one whom she had to seek out in a different world—
but not a favoured figure among those who loved and
prized her. Whether his presence in her life made more
for her happiness or the reverse there was only one person, herself, who ever knew, and the knowledge died
with her—if even she had ever known.

He was an insatiable reader, a true glutton of books;
he was a hard worker, with a wide acquaintance among
men of learning and letters and affairs; he was a good
linguist, and a traveller who searched and mastered the

art and culture of many lands. As a critic, a student, a tourist, he shared with Edith many enterprises after her heart, and his practical experience helped her in difficult times. This on the right side. On the other there was very plainly the harshness of a dogmatist, the bleakness of an egotist, and the pretentiousness (I can't help it) of a snob; and from all these she suffered hurts in her growth that were lasting. Thus it came about that she was to be left high and dry, for many a long year to come, upon the established rationalism of his day; and there she sat on, refusing to argue about a closed subject, while the queries and researches of the following days were so insidiously reopening it. She seemed to think that 'doubt,' a half-way house between materialist orthodoxy and religious, was still, from whichever side approached, the same makeshift and consoling refuge that it was for tender souls in Tennysonian times—and she would have none of that. On these matters I must wait for the help of others, which will not be wanting later on. Enough just now to recall how she used to brush aside speculation, upsetting the table of argument the moment it was set for anything that looked like a philosophical debate. The lively leap of her mind stopped dead when she was asked to think, I don't say only about the meaning and the ends of life, but almost about any theoretic enquiry, any fanciful rearrangement of the world as it appears; social and political guesswork (she wouldn't allow it to be more) was bundled away as easily as any other. It was a check on her spirit that seemed a violation of its native freedom, and so it was. There came indeed a day of many changes in this order; but that day was still in the far distance, and meanwhile it is not to be supposed that we know Edith Wharton unless we know the man who so predominated among those who peopled and furnished her life. He will not, he shall not, be seen again in this book till the time comes to take leave of him; but he will be there throughout, an unforgotten presence in the background. He was an international lawyer of high repute, and the greater part of his career was divided between important appointments, first at Washington, later at Cairo, and finally in Paris, where he died in 1927.

Of other friends, older and younger, who helped her, each in his place, to discover herself as a writer of books, there is one left * of the older to speak of her as he saw her then. Judge Robert Grant, author of *Unleavened Bread*, the novel which she admired and recognised as the forerunner of the 'American school' of later days, allows me to quote some pages from a commemorative address lately read by him before the American Academy of Arts and Letters in New York.

My long friendship with Edith Wharton dates from very shortly after her marriage. We had previously exchanged a letter or two, but the first time I met her was at Groton, where she was visiting with her husband at the house of a mutual friend. Teddy Wharton was thirteen years her senior, a friend of my boyhood and a college class-mate. I was struck by his bride's refinement, but was kept a little aloof at first by her reserve—for even as late as this she suffered in the presence of strangers from what she has termed 'the long cold agony of shyness.' Because Charles Scribner was my own publisher I had the opportunity to observe her modest,

* He died in 1940, since this was written.

[45]

yet wonderfully swift development under the discernment of Edward L. Burlingame, editor of the magazine, and his colleague William C. Brownell, adviser of the publishing house. They accepted her first short stories, recognising in them the touch of a new artist in letters. There was an interval of only two years between her venture, *The Decoration of Houses,* written with Ogden Codman, and the appearance of *The Greater Inclination* (1899), the book of short stories which caused the London bookseller to say to Mrs. Wharton, not knowing who she was, as he handed it to her, 'This is what everyone in London is talking about now.' Three years later appeared her first novel, *The Valley of Decision* . . . and three years later again (1905) *The House of Mirth,* that compelling yet touching satire on New York society as it was within the memory of many who read it, and Mrs. Wharton's reputation as a fearless and veracious artist was made. . . .

Because of our kindred tastes I was one of the group who from time to time visited at The Mount, delighting in its abundant hospitality and the sparkling talk we heard there. The group was small and of different ages. It was a trait of the hostess to like devotedly the people she fancied and disregard the outer world. Even then and oftener in the years to come I heard her spoken of as cold and unpatriotic. But invariably it was by women who did not approve of her analytic mind. . . . My last visit to The Mount seemed the happiest at the moment, for each of my hosts gave the impression of being in love with what they builded, and Edith spoke gleefully of hoping to pay for a new terrace with the profits of her next book. Within three weeks I heard they had decided to uproot themselves and live abroad. The decision seemed a mystery at the time. Teddy Wharton was an attractive man, debonair, spruce, and amiable; they had many fastidious tastes in common, but he was not intellectual, and his wife had in this sense outgrown him. We have Edith's printed word for it that his growing ill-health was the underlying cause of their emigration. On the other hand the lure of Europe and wider literary associations were fully understandable as one of her motives, and at the moment it seemed as if Teddy would find the boulevards of Paris thoroughly congenial. But he never fitted in, and they bored him. On the other hand her eager intelligence derived fresh vigour and atmosphere from the old world and from the contacts her growing reputation brought her. . . . In 1909 she wrote me: 'It is curious that when I was younger and busy with my own slow development, I could subsist on *myself* indefinitely, with only a vague unformulated need of companionship *de l'esprit;* whereas now I find myself greatly stimulated by it, and consequently more and more dependent on having it for at least a few months of each year. Hence my great enjoyment of London and Paris.'

Certainly, as Judge Grant hints, it is not necessary to look far, nor even as far as she looks herself, for the reason why she began to edge more and more towards Europe in these days—not merely for plunges and excursions, which had never ceased to be regularly made, but for a yearly settlement of some months. (For several years it was not more than that, and The Mount saw her again each summer.) It was clear enough that 'great enjoyment' in Paris and London was hers for the taking, and not surprising, since there was nothing to hinder her, that she should proceed to take it. As for profounder reasons—such as the need of wider or richer fields of observation for the growing avidity of her art— these too it would be easy to find, and possibly more than are in strictness required. There was no such pull of desire in her as there had been years before in young Henry James, no such hunger for a world ancient and solid enough to stand the pressure of an imagination that never rested; she was a diligent worker, to be sure, but not as massively earnest as all that. And yet it is true, no doubt, if with more truth than the particular case demands, that America in those days was quaking ground for a novelist.

> When she made her move [Mr. G. Lapsley at this point interposes] she was to all appearance standing (in America) between two worlds, 'one dead, the other powerless to be born.' The old social organisation was in dissolution, and the society in which she worked, still socially and economically well placed, was in process of being pushed eastward and across the Atlantic; and the time was not yet when anyone could dare to affirm that the old American tradition could maintain, even with notable modifications, its continuous American identity.

This is history, seen in the making by an historian's eye; and if a novelist is to be justified for abandoning her home, here is her warrant. And in fact she did feel always a little on her defence against the charge—frequently made, I gather, and not without acrimony—that she was an unnatural daughter of her country; and there is even a touch of self-consciousness in the excuse she alleged, looking back long afterwards, for her original flight. There was more in it all than her husband's health, if there was less than Mr. Lapsley offers her; and perhaps after all she might be allowed to enjoy herself greatly.

She came to Europe, then, by degrees and stages, not propelled by a great decision. She was not in the least the 'passionate pilgrim' of Henry James, transferring the allegiance of a yearning heart, restored to its spiritual home. She had no cause to regard herself, nor yet to be regarded, as in need of any teaching or blessing from another world. She came to Europe bearing her own illumination with her, to meet the best that others could bring to match it. She came, let us put it in a word, for talk—for more talk with more people, and with people as fearless of talk, as familiar with it, as dependent on it, as herself. She had made her own space for talk at home, as much as she could, and had filled it well with her chosen band. But if, scouring the country, she had collected a houseful that could give her what she wanted, in Paris the house became a city, a kingdom—and how was she to refuse it? And of course, for the matter of that, her talent was bound to revel in research wherever it was placed, and more so than ever in deeper acquaintance with these more beaten and footprinted ways of the world; and if Europe was to provide her with more novels to be written, so much the better for us all. But it was not as a seeker, not as a votary, not as a strayed exile that she came to us; no such illusion is permitted us in the case of Edith Wharton. She came to enjoy what had long been hers at home, only she had not enough of it—the best society within view, the best talk within earshot: not always to be found within the same four walls, no doubt, but soon to be brought together within her own. She never became, she had no call to become, any more of a European than she had been from the first; but with Europe around her she had room, liberty, encouragement, to be what she was.

IV

Paris: friendship and talk

She spoke just now of her pleasure in the company of London and Paris, but of course it was Paris that really came first, with London for a long while far behind. There may have been a time, later on, when she wished, or nearly wished, that she had followed the example of her precursor and had taken England for her province; there was even a moment when she thought of doing so after all. And indeed the reasons that had been good for the earlier case had surely been good for hers too. The roots of a colonist from across the ocean, give them time, are likely to be found deeper in English soil than they would ever have penetrated in any other; and I have tried to imagine how Edith would have appeared at last if she had taken possession of English life with the concentration and application of Henry James. But if baffles imagination; for the fact is that in the days when the choice was open she could never have admitted the very simple, but quite indisputable, English terms. Too easy indeed for words, as they seem to us: and yet we all know how much less amusing it is, or was in youth, to make new friends within the family than beyond it; for within the circle of the blood they are too apt to accept you naturally, to take you for granted, and new friendships, to be interesting, should create more circumstance and need more care. It may be a little flat, in short, to find yourself treated as one of the family from the first moment of arrival, with no more stir to it than that. A stranger in our midst will begin, we must admit it, with exasperation in the fellowship of a race whose margin of indifference (or should I say insensibility?—or might I say tolerance?) is so great that they apparently don't even notice the difficulties, delicate and delightful, in the art of making friends—they let it happen, neither giving nor expecting explanations. But then at last, no longer a stranger, he may come to feel that no company in the world is easier than that which regards him kindly and calmly as a matter of course—as an old and familiar habit. That is the English way, too simple for words; and even Edith may have felt, as life went on, that the English way can be a comfort at times. But in the days of the fulness of her energy there could be no question: it was Paris for her.

It must be the right Paris, however: by no means the city of the general settler from overseas, where he installs himself among his kind and calls it Paris. Not in any quarter of new smartness, of spruce and polyglot modernity—in a very different region is the place for one who looks for the best in the art of manners and communications. Across the river, in the discreet old recesses of the Faubourg—more and more penned, the fate of distinction everywhere, in a shrinking space encroached upon from all around—tradition, noble and composed, still lives, or did still live when this affinity from the new world brought to it her fine understanding of its quality. The narrow streets, the retiring 'cités,' the closed portals of the great houses within their courts, the tree-tops leaning over the walls of their hidden gardens—among these is the spot, if you are seeking for the heart of civilisation, where you end your journey. France in the world (if all the world is open to you), Paris in France, and the Faubourg St. Germain in Paris—you can evidently go no farther; and a dignified apartment in the Rue de Varenne, with a row of rooms looking towards the sober and elegant privacy of the past behind it, will be a home to abide in.* It was not in the event an abiding home for Edith Wharton, but her life was centred there for a number of years—years fruitful in work and interest, years shadowed by troubles and anxieties of her own, years finally overarched by the vast cloud of war; and through them all it was a true home to her, suiting her with a 'grace of congruity,' perfectly becoming to her style. The noise of the boulevards was very far away. It seemed like an excursion to set forth in the morning for a visit to that other Paris of clatter and glitter, and strange to find it there so soon— and strange again to leave it so easily and return in a few minutes to the silvery calm of so different a world.

Here then she lived at last in plenty. She had all the company about her that she needed, and of all the kinds; and so long as her company was right of its kind she was not exclusive, and there was a great deal of variety to be seen in her charming rooms. Only this was always certain, that nothing admitted to the mixture would appear out of place against the background of her creation; the careless or the formless were no more to be found there than the rough or the rude. It was ever a polite gathering; but all were there who could interest Edith

---

* I am thinking of the house, 53 Rue de Varenne, where nearly all her Parisian life was spent. There was a short prelude in another house, on the opposite side of the same street.

Wharton, and the ways of interesting her were many and diverse. Between the worldly and the literary lay her range, touching no far extreme in either direction; and within these limits, talent not too unworldly, elegance not too illiterate, there was space for a large concourse, and it was admirably filled. And sure enough, since this was Paris, they could all talk—how indeed should they *not* talk, as Henry James remarked, with such an instrument at their command, the violin of the French tongue, on which everyone played with the 'bowing arm' of a virtuoso. And again, here in Paris she found prepared for her a world of men—a society in which the men were as plentiful and as civilised as the women, to say the least of it. More than one of her friends have already noted, without surprise, that she preferred the company of men; and indeed there were some obvious reasons why she should, two of the more so being that she had a very feminine consciousness and a very masculine mind. She liked to be surrounded by the suit of an attentive court, and she liked to be talked to as a man; and both likings were gratified in a world of men and talk. And there was another reason too, not quite so obvious. The friendships that will go far and last long with a little impersonal dryness in them, the salt of independence, were those in which she was happy, and it was mainly with men that she found them.

She felt perhaps safer with men—safer from the claims and demands of a personal relation: from some of which she shrank so instinctively that intimacy, what most people would call intimacy, was to her of the last difficulty. One of the women who knew her best, an old friend and contemporary, recalls and confirms what Paul Bourget always said of her, 'To understand Edith one must recognise that she is *une sensitive'*—so much so that the presence and proximity of people, were they even the most familiar of friends, seemed to check or chill her response, and to the end they might scarcely know, unless sometimes her letters showed them, that she needed and returned their warmth. It is hard to speak of a chill, a check upon the swiftness of the sympathy that so many found in her; but certainly those who looked to her for a flow of deep communion, heart speaking to heart—and I suppose they might be mostly women—wouldn't find it. Anyhow *une sensitive* she was, to whom the contiguity of the human world, the vicinity of all that mass of conscious being, was dread as well as delight, and in every peck of interest there were grains of terror. This, I cannot doubt, was the greater part (not quite all) of the explanation of her famous 'shyness,' of which we have heard and shall hear more— and which certainly wasn't shyness as most of us know it, merely faltering and forlorn. That familiar misery is easily dispelled—by kindness, merely encouraging and warm; and as for kindness, as for encouragement, it was not these that would serve to put Edith at her ease. *She* was kind, *she* was welcoming and reassuring, if you like—or if *she* liked; but I don't see another consoling her fears by such mild means. The way to her confidence was through free converse, direct communication, open companionship, with all the intimacy that doesn't cling or bind, not more. Is that no intimacy at all? Answers evidently differ; but no friend of hers didn't deeply prize her friendship. There was, to be sure, one other condition to be satisfied in approaching her; you *must* realise that a person in her position has her position to think of—not indeed for a moment that of a woman of

[55]

celebrated talent, which could easily take care of itself, but that of a lady who, as the poet says, was *such* a lady. Social place must first be recognised, then given its due; and this was always the other little preoccupation in her reception, never quite unguarded, of the thronging world.

'Ah, my dear young man, you have made friends with Edith Wharton. I congratulate you. You may find her difficult, but you will find nothing stupid in her and nothing small.' The speaker was Henry James, once more—and I like to think how he and Bourget watched over her on either hand, those two great analytical observers, 'bending one way their precious influence.' (The young man was John Hugh-Smith, but he awaits me elsewhere.) Difficult, oh yes: but all is well and easy wherever the intelligence of the company is quick and the critical tone is high. The game of conversation delighted her, and she was a match for the best in it; and the game served till the real thing appeared, but not a moment longer. There was no trifling when serious fare of the right kind was on the board. I don't know whether she fell on it more avidly when it was talk about people or talk about books; but in any case the tone, remember, must find and keep its height. She may talk by the hour about people, their manners and customs, their scrapes and scandals, so long as these throw light upon the chase of human nature, fit quarry for a noble curiosity. There is of course also the mere clack that takes its interest only from the personal names it worries, but this soon drops—though not, I own, till she has snatched out the laugh that is in it, sweet or sharp. And then to books, to ideas, to the trail of human imagination: it is an easy extension into all her reading, her travelling, her enquiring, soon girdling the globe. Blank tracts there will be, we already know—dark continents that may appeal to you, where she is not to be enticed; but her raids and dashing piracies and masterly settlements in so many a quarter are quite enough entertainment for to-day—for a hundred days. And the tone, remember still!—the tone can't be maintained save where criticism rules; and her standard in criticism is ever the same, true to its mark. On that level, on none lower, the talk runs with a swing and a lift in it, throwing itself forward from point to point: talk that flings out and glances wide, not peers or burrows. And when it ends as it began, in an explosion of fun, none of the highest, in which decorum is blown out of window, all the more surely it is the talk of Edith Wharton enjoying herself among her friends.

Certainly, among her friends [Gaillard Lapsley again intervenes, very much to the point]: but her conversation in society, particularly when she was receiving, was a different matter. You see she was immensely shy [yes, yes!]—but many people did not know that, because she was in no sense timid. (It wasn't wholly a matter of natural courage, though she had plenty of that in all conscience, but partly because she did not know what it was to be poor, and to have to put up with the best you could afford and be satisfied with it. If you have always paid handsomely for the best that can be had, you don't scruple to make a row because it isn't better—at any rate Edith never did.) Then people she did not know well, more especially continental Europeans, had the double effect of embarrassing and intoxicating her. Confronted by a room full of them she became a different person—or rather showed herself in an induced state. Her talk was neither unnatural nor insincere—on the contrary, it was characteristic and witty, but intensified by a stimulus as exhausting in its reaction as it was exhilarating at the time. You were left in no doubt about that if you watched her unconscious manoeuvres—from time to time she would shift her seat, straighten her back and fill her lungs, *se rengorgeant* for a fresh effort. She had the concentration of intense enjoyment and interest and a responsible consciousness of the whole scene— from what her guests were saying and how they were reacting, down to the delay of the footman in bringing back the tea-kettle she had sent to be refilled. But such talk cost her an effort disproportionate to the occasion, though I don't think that it seemed strained or unnatural to those who did not know her well—and for that very reason. Then behind it all there was the rather anxious hostess cumbered with many cares and trying to look after everything—who, if she saw you smoke after tea when everyone had refused, would rebuke you by pointedly asking you to pass the cigarettes. All this was extremely exhausting, and it became the more so if you recall the temperamental restlessness which raged under restraint.

To the vivid truth of this glimpse of her 'in society' there is nothing to add; I follow the eyes of this friend, who knew her so well, and recognise it all. We see her, it is to be understood, entertaining in her own house (as the guest of others she had a much easier time) a company for which she feels a special responsibility—as a hostess, and as a foreign hostess at that. It would have been simpler if she hadn't been so versed in the geography, so to speak, of society and its ways. She knew France too well to engage it lightly, as an innocent smatterer might in her place. Her care betrayed itself in more ways than one—and one was her perceptible anxiety lest her English-speaking friends (who have smiled at it) should expose themselves as too painfully home-bred. (I may mention, by the way, that her French as she spoke it was fully as free and agile as her English, though never in intonation the speech of France.) And again it was betrayed by the prompt relaxation of her tension when the company had dispersed—when she could quit the stage and throw up her part and say what she liked to her friends. The blest relief!—we can all sympathise with her there, but with a certain wonder. For this was Edith whom none could bind, who chose her own way and stood no dictation from the world; and here she was exhausting herself gratuitously in a world for which, whatever the tongue it happened to speak, she professed not the slightest respect. What did it give her to reward her pains? Well, no doubt it is exhilarating to stretch your powers and work your talents to their utmost, in any field of exercise; and even in soil of which you have no high opinion there may be a buried moidore. But on the whole it was enough that wherever a social world was in sight, duly accredited, a place there must be in it as of right for Edith Wharton; and she must take it, and there was no more to be said. It was truly a different matter when she was not 'receiving,' or not what could be called society; and now she is with her friends again, sharing and embellishing their ease.

With all this she was still leading that other life, the life in her work, and giving good proof, year by year, of its intensity, though it was always a marvel where she hid it. Her books, growing in the privacy of which there seemed to be so little, appeared in their succession with increasing freedom and assurance—the books of a writer who evidently loved every moment of her work and every nicety of her craft. 'Look at her,' said somebody once, watching her in her drawing-room, trim and alert in her panoply: 'who would think she had ever written a line—with that figure?' It was ingenuously said; but we can turn the saying round and ask who would ever think, reading her books, that they were written in the bare margin of such a populous and ornamental existence. They are a writer's books, displaying in perfect composure the sleight of the writer's hand—books that look straight in the face of professional criticism, obviously caring for none other. The scarce hours of seclusion in which they grew must have been well muffled against the noise without; and indeed they were, and by more than a door strictly closed. Her work was not her life—it had to fit in with very much else, and she cut out nothing for its sake; but it was her faith, the expression of her firmest and clearest belief. She believed in her art, the art she ensued with every master of it—believed in it once for all, with a single mind; and wherever it appeared, everything else gave way at the mention of its name. She had never the doubt of a moment; if a word should be ventured that implied a slight to it— a treachery to the calling of the artist, the man who makes truth out of life—she swept it aside as a triviality to which she couldn't listen. With this conviction, perfect and final, her work was secure, though it had but its accorded place and must keep to it.

I have to turn to another matter, a less happy one—that began as a disquietude, a shade of apprehension, deepening gradually and at last rapidly into sore trouble and agitation. I have hitherto left it to others to speak of Edward Wharton, my own knowledge of him being of the slightest; and others have said enough to show him clearly in his broad geniality, his easy contentment with the pleasant lines of his existence, his pride in the brilliance of his wife. 'There was the stuff in him,' says G. L., 'for a real friendly companionship with Edith, and she had the less difficulty in creating it that it was, I suspect, the relation with men that she understood best.' More than this for her part it doubtless never was, but it was fully this, and it meant the sharing through many years of the most, if not the best, of the contents of her life. She made no slight demands on his patience and indulgence; but then he had large resources of his own in these kinds, at any rate where she and her activities and enjoyments were concerned. And he, very likely, made equal demands on her, where of those particular resources she had much less; but then the breadth of her reason and her appreciation supplied the lack. He was the man who represented unquestioning kindness and loyalty in her life, always on her side as a matter of course—help that to a critical spirit may be a rarer comfort in the long run than even the finest comprehension. He was (as I think G. L. implies) the right kind of husband for her, if she could have but one; for she saw and said herself that she needed several, if the whole of her life was to be shared and enhanced by another. Enough, it was a good alliance, with unflagging interest in it for one partner, trusted support for the other—for each a need generously fulfilled; and it held firm for many years, and might indeed have continued to hold, if an unexpected strain, the fault of neither, had not been thrown upon it in course of time.

'A shadow, slight at first and then increasing, fell across The Mount in the last years that she lived there.' It is again Mr. Updike who speaks, as he spoke before, with full knowledge and understanding; and the reader is reminded that these first Parisian winters were balanced by summers of the old sort at Lenox.

Her marriage until then had been a happy one; but an infirmity of temper grew on Mr. Wharton, unreasoning anger about trifles, which at first puzzled, then worried, finally disturbed Edith beyond measure. Perhaps if the fact that there was some tendency to mental disturbance had been recognised earlier, if the right word at the right moment had been spoken, or if the Lenox house had not been sold, the rift would not have widened and the final separation might not have come to pass. I felt the disposal of The Mount deeply, discouraged it in such slight ways as I could, and feared the consequences—more for him than for her. He was devoted to the country; the place at Lenox (where he had passed much of his boyhood) was a constant amusement, and his love of animals and country life gave him deep roots in the soil. To her the change to Paris opened vistas of artistic pleasure and intellectual development; but for him it took away his chief occupations, and he found himself stranded in a society for which he was neither adapted nor inclined. Add to this an illness partly nervous and partly mental, and it is easy to understand the grave differences that later on came between them.

There need be no dwelling on the details of this long unhappiness; they were known to few, and that it came at last to the only possible issue was questioned, I believe, by none who fully knew them. Nor was it ever doubted, by those who best knew her, that it was no failure of sympathy or courage on her part that brought her at length to her decision; great courage and true feeling she had shown throughout—the end must else have come much sooner. As ever in such cases, there were many vicissitudes in the progress of her husband's malady; and it was when her generosity and forbearance were most heavily tried that she proved the truth of her friend's word—'there was nothing small in her.' Whatever could be done she did; the severance from her American home may have been, as Mr. Updike suggests, a mistake in judgment, but it seems that for this she was not herself responsible. By 1912 things had reached a point where it was evident that no effort or sacrifice of hers could any further avail, and the separation that ensued became a divorce in the following year. Thenceforward her home was in France, and she crossed the ocean but once again, and that only after many years. So it fell out, but not because there was any bitterness, born of these troubles, in her thoughts of old days. Of that there was no trace in her at any time; and I have been told by a friend who knew and saw him later that there was even touchingly none in Mr. Wharton, till his death in 1928. In the good will of friendship they were well and equally matched.

V

English ways

France was her home, but it was in England that she could take a holiday. She felt no responsibility for the English in their own island, and whenever she crossed the Channel it was to enjoy the best time they could give her, with no other care on her mind. I think they gave her good recreation. If their art in entertainment was unstudied, they could at least welcome her warmly into the freedom of their loose and open order; and the unoppressive go-as-you-please of their social ways made an informal playground of London after the organised perfection of her home. England, as I said before, may receive a new friend with provoking calm, but on the other hand it offers this advantage, that you can drop in on England at any moment, without warning, and be taken into the party on the spot, without ceremony. And a visitor such as this, who doesn't wait to be drawn out (or she might wait long), but who colours the scene and kindles the talk from the moment she enters the room—who sheds a festal light on every gathering (if it is to her mind) that she joins—is it likely that this visitor will not be acclaimed and made much of whenever she chooses to appear? She took her holiday in London with increasing freedom as the years went on, and the shade of reserve, of fastidious disparagement, with which she seemed to regard London some time ago, on an earlier page, vanished in intercourse with a circle of friends that widened with every visit. London as a massive institution, as a huge pile of national life and work and state—that was one thing; but quite another was London of the easily opening doors and the casual hospitality and the nonchalant amenity that were the note of the circle in which she found her friends. I don't say it was a world that could have satisfied her for long, with the old and offhand please-yourself which is at the bottom of its character; but for a holiday it had many attractions.

And then in England there were always those two retreats of joyous intimacy, at Rye and at Windsor, to fall back upon; and so we bring her again to the friends with whom we first saw her, better able now than in that dazzled hour to measure what they found in her society. By this time we quite see why to Henry James she was so shining a 'case'—and also why, with all his pride in her, he was apt to deplore what might seem to be her levity in tackling the case of England. For it was all very well, the informality of England was certainly a large part of it, but an earnest student soon finds a great deal more than that upon his hands in this land of adventurers so conservative, of home-lovers so vagrant, playing or toiling at their work or their play, you can scarcely say which. If you don't go deeper into English life (says Henry James, by the by) than the happy inconsequence of a few favoured hours, what do you make of the questions with which it bristles for an attentive imagination? He shook his head at the monstrosity of her freedom. I remember one day at Qu'acre, when Howard Sturgis, turning the pages of her latest story (it was *Ethan Frome*), read out a passing remark of the fictitious narrator's—'I had been sent by my employers'; and how Henry caught at the words, with his great round stare of drollery and malice at the suggested image—of Edith *sent,* and sent by *employers!*—what a power of invention it implied in her to think of that! Alas, there could be no such fortunate compulsion for Edith outside her story. He was distressed by her lightning reversals and rearrangements of settled plans. How are you ever to know where you are, if, wherever you are, you can *always* change your mind and go elsewhere? 'Here we are—and now it begins to rain—let's be off—why not try the south of France?' What becomes of experience, saturation, discrimination, if you are as free as that?

Well, but she was holiday-making; and whatever he said he was glad to go with her and to chance the weather when she carried him round the country in her motor-car. For we are now looking back to the early years when the motor was a luxury that had renewed the romance of travel, releasing the tourist from the tyranny of the line, restoring him to the liberty of the road; and the happy car-owner, embracing the landscape at his own good time and will, was borne back to the spacious days of the grand tour, but with a mobility beyond any dream of his ancestors. Edith had fallen upon the new plaything as though it had been invented for her. She saw at once how to make the right use of it; she claimed its service, its blind obedience to her command, and it was her slave from the first. While others were still petting or humouring it, adapting their ways to its pride or its whims, she had grasped it with a clear understanding, not indeed of the mere machinery of its action, for which she cared nothing, but of the opportunity of its power. She trailed the cloud of her dust along the open highways, she threaded the green lanes that were still startled by the strange new beast; and though the dust was soon laid, the white road blackened, and the hoot of the horn as familiar as the cuckoo's cry, she remained an example to all for the intelligence with which she worked the capacity of her slave. It played its honourable, never obtrusive or assertive part in innumerable excursions; I should like to see a map of England, France, Italy—of half Europe and more— that should be marked with the track of her wheels from first to last. Very often indeed it was Henry who sat with her to watch, what he adored, the large unfolding of the countryside as they swept across it. She mentioned once that the car in which they were riding had been bought with the proceeds of her last novel. 'With the proceeds of *my* last novel,' said Henry meditatively, 'I purchased a small go-cart, or hand-barrow, on which my guests' luggage is wheeled from the station to my house. It needs a coat of paint. With the proceeds of my next I shall have it painted.' But if the Golden Bowl was skimped, there was always a place for him in the House of Mirth.

I chance to see her set forth next with a new companion, occupying that place; and now I own that I watch her departure with a rueful eye. For John Hugh-Smith remembers and handsomely acknowledges that *he* found his way into her car and company by means of a friend of his who was left on the doorstep (but he was used to that) when they whirled away; and whereas the friend was still doubtfully screwing up his courage to attract her attention, John, much readier and braver, had established his place with her in one evening, when he joined, and so luminously and substantially enriched, the talk at Qu'acre. That was the sort of young Englishman she needed, a most unusual sort; for the ideas that thronged in his brain weren't imprisoned there, they streamed out in lively order; and he knew so many books, and so much life as well, that in a very short time they were talking at each other as though they couldn't stop. There was no call for them to stop, when he was invited to stay beside her during her progress through the land; they could talk in the car, rather to the neglect of the landscape, till they descended at her next destination, whichever it was: she seemed, by report, to be moving from one stately home to another after she left us at Qu'acre. And later on, when John rejoined his friend, it was John who could tell his friend so much about Edith that he still couldn't stop, and again no reason why he should when his tale was so interesting; and so we discussed her, admired her, criticised her, and generally and finally agreed that she was a wonder. John, boldly experienced, could place her in her right position from many points of view—literary, social, racial, personal; and his range of illustration gave form and substance to a vision dazzling indeed, but farther than ever beyond the reach of shyness (the real thing!) when she passed away into the world of her natural affinities. There might be little left that I didn't know about her now, but I seemed no nearer to knowing Edith.

The world of her affinities, clearly to be discerned in John's striking exposition, was a world as free as herself, with all the grace of emancipation and none of its harshness. It was a warm and nimble air that was circulating in those beautiful haunts. What splendid houses, what exquisite entertainment, what brisk-witted gaiety!—I could easily picture the scene. Glad they must be, those happy folk, to beguile the leisure of their distinguished visitor and to court her with their spells. But the integrity of youth, safely screened from these temptations, is severe; nobly disinterested in its concern for the serious artist, it mistrusts for her the garden of Armida. It may ask how a woman of such exacting judgment can be content with company in which art is an amusement, not a life to be lived. Didn't she realise that the true makers of art and shapers of thought were to be found elsewhere—that those who could read and understand her aright were awaiting her where she had failed to observe them, perhaps on the very doorstep from which she had launched her flight? One can't say such things aloud: pride forbids —and Howard would smile with too much penetration; but they grumble in the mind, encouraging a reasonable—and so altruistic!—sense of grievance. Isn't it the highest tribute to her art to feel that her place is with the workers, not the players? Moreover, when she does reappear among those she had left behind, one gathers that she hasn't been impressed by the level of intellect in the garden; not a little sport is made of the ingenuous ideas that prevail there. But does she then think she has been listening to the best we have to offer? Must we conclude that she won't go where thought is rich but entertainment modest? Dare one suppose that she has been a little spoilt by the world, and that the ranks of the toilers aren't fine enough for her? It may be so. But how upright, how high-minded, how incorruptible is youth when it has failed to be interesting!

She too had her failures, though she didn't brood over them; for her attempts, when she made any, to discover the treasures I speak of weren't always rewarded. It was no fault of hers but she did arrive, wherever she alighted, as such an event; and it had to be confessed that she looked out of place in homely surroundings. And well she might, and what matter?—only she seemed to be aware of it herself, and that was the trouble. The whisper of a question ran round, not inaudibly: why must Mrs. Wharton be treated as royalty? None knew why, but all were conscious that she must, and not unnaturally it didn't make for ease. Let us clear out of this delicate imbroglio and abandon the effort, once for all, to bring her into circles where the arrival of royalty is an event; it will never work. But first wait one moment for a little picture that rises before me in sharp detail as I write, from thirty years ago. The scene is a small London drawing-room, a very small one; and here at any rate there was a rich nugget of character and crackle of wit to be discovered, for it was the room in which Rhoda Broughton sat to receive her friends. Edith must on no account leave London— Howard was firm on the point—without making the acquaintance of Miss Broughton: an historic name, so far in the Victorian past had the comedy of her fiction begun to flower; and now in her advancing years, with her comedy matured to an astringent flavour all its own, a figure of rare mark and brave stamp as ever you might see. Rhoda was equal to any event, and she took her own way, very direct, with any and all. But were she to suspect that she was on view as a show, as a sight that a distinguished visitor mustn't miss, Rhoda's back, never a pliable one, would stiffen, her wit shut down with a snap, her fine old ease narrow to a cramped politeness, her elbows tighten at her sides. And now we see Edith in the opposite chair, warm and bright and attentive, as she wrought her best to pierce the defence and win the countenance of this difficult British maiden. She really tried, but in vain; the distinction of her visit was not to be disguised, nor Rhoda to be sweetened by even the most tactful of favours. It is hard that the proffer of graciousness should fail when it is meant in all sincerity to please; but I say it will never work.

And now at last, after these discouraging delays, that happened which had seemed impossible. There was more left to know about Edith than I had supposed, and by good fortune the chance to learn it was at hand—no farther off than Cambridge, as I might surely have discovered sooner. When Gaillard Lapsley, early in the century, left America to settle in Cambridge he brought with him, no doubt, much that was fresh and new to the university and to his college, for their profit; and one thing in particular he brought that may not have stirred his college, but to me, a very constant visitor to Cambridge and Trinity and G. L., it was of the most fruitful concern. He brought the possession of an old and easy acquaintance with Edith Wharton. He had known her at home, in her American days, in her native air, and he seemed to know her differently from the rest of us—to know her as no one could who only beheld her as an event, a meteor from overseas, spreading her train. He appeared by contrast to know her quietly and privately, and when he talked of her the tone struck me; he seemed, even before he admired and applauded her, to be fond of her. I had heard very much of her as a marvel and seen not a little of her as a vision; and now she was appearing as a familiar companion, bound by kindly associations—you might say simply as a friend. It was as though an illumination were extinguished and daylight admitted; and it was singular to see, and pleasant too, how her expression changed. No one need be afraid of her now; she liked the kindness of a friend, she even needed it. Daylight, mildly diffused, is more to be trusted than a thousand lamps to show a true likeness. It might be hard to know what to make of certain contradictions and discrepancies between the two views; and I may say that it *was* hard, to the end, to reconcile all that was to be seen in her with the whole of her. She was not one who always dwelt at the centre of herself and was always to be found there; and her migrations, the shifts of her consistency, never ceased to be confounding. But when once she had been discovered in the light that showed her as a friend, alone with a friend, this was the discovery that prevailed; and now we can proceed in that light.

I had proceeded far, however it happened, by the date of my next picture, which belongs to the summer of 1913. I was in the car with her now, and G. L. too, and we were driving into the country, in high July weather, for an interesting purpose. It was the year in which, as I have shown, a change had been brought about in Edith Wharton's life by a decision finally taken, accomplished, and laid away into the past in silence, there to remain. It was natural that then, if ever, the tie with Paris should be loosened and a new one made with England—at any rate that England should give her a settled home of her own in summer, to replace The Mount. And so we drove into Essex to inspect an old house recommended to her notice. An interesting place it was too, set round with cedars and walled gardens, dignified in desertion and neglect: a place that cried out for a sympathetic hand to repair its beauty—and why not Edith's? It seemed to me a clear call; but she wasn't sure. She was attracted by England and the old house, but I now think that when it came to the point she was afraid—not of the house, for she would have loved to give the sweet and forlorn old place the care that was its due, but in a manner afraid of England. Wouldn't it be safer to keep England as it was, holiday-ground for which she had no responsibility—to leave well alone, where it was now so very well? The question, a pressing one as we made our inspection of the place and were moved by its appeal, hung unanswered when we left and continued to hang for some time to come: and I believe in the end it might have been answered in favour of the house after all, if next year's July, with the abhorred shears, had not slit the thread of this pretty hope with all the rest. When plans and hopes were possible again, after the years of war, she found and was committed to others—very good plans too, as they turned out, and rewarding hopes. But I return in thought to the old white house among the cedars and the deserted gardens that dipped to the reedy lake, and still see the life that we pictured her creating there, and resign it with regret. Edith with a home of her own in England was a sight that beckoned us kindly for an hour, and I shall always wish we could have had more of it.

That same evening she bore us off (both of us!) on a visit to friends of hers in the neighbourhood. Here was a great house indeed, standing high in glory on its hill, stately in charm, genial in splendour, where hospitality was as large and serene as the summer sky. And now I could see for myself how Edith entered a great house of friends and how she was welcomed there, and I saw more than I expected. I saw her, I can see her still, rustling forward with her quick step, hitching her scarf round her shoulders, advancing into the midst of the vast hall and the scattered company with a smile of embracing familiarity, with flying looks and side glances of understanding —with an air of amused and confidential anticipation, as of one in league with youth and fun and freedom. Simpler, easier, younger than I had ever seen her before, without a care on her mind among people who had none on theirs, without a strain on her resources among people who didn't tax their own: it was wholesome company for Edith. She had a rallying, challenging way with the elders of the party that was not to be resisted, and with the younger sort the happiest way of all, an equality in laughter and curiosity that caught and won them out of hand. This was Edith when she hadn't an effort to make, nor anything to maintain or to answer for—where friendliness happened around her of its own accord. As for the company, it was one in which friendliness happened so often and so naturally that there could be nothing in that evening to surprise them; and all they saw or expected to see was Edith as charming and amusing as ever. Such and no more were their arts, the spells they wove to entertain her; it was a white and simple magic. But of Hill Hall and its welcome, of Mary Hunter and her family and their free-handed ways, I mustn't now begin to talk; I only describe how they found what they expected in their visitor.

But the quickest and directest way of all to her confidence was even simpler; it was no more than the twinkle of an eye. If her glance met another's at the right moment, in mutual understanding, the thing was done;

and the right moment was when she and another were amused by the same stroke, and each detected an ally. Whatever touched the hair-trigger of her joy in absurdity found her primed for laughter, and she hailed an ally who understood. 'She never failed,' says G. L., changing my figure, 'to rise to a fly that was fantastic or absurd. She would laugh with the sincerity of complete surrender to every paroxysm that followed a fresh vision of the ludicrous that she caught or was offered. I can see her, speechless with shoulders shaking and the tears running down her cheeks, lift a deprecating hand that bade you spare her another turn of the screw, or at least "give her ribs of steel." ' When laughter attacked her (for yet another figure) she surrendered at discretion; and the laughter she loved best was the point-blank kind, straight in the face, that will take no denial. The skilful cut of wit she also enjoyed, and was very deft at it herself; but that is a different enjoyment, in which the brain still holds its own and keeps its step. The play of humour too: but hers was not really a humourous view of life, if humour is tolerant and contemplative; she was too quick and practical to give humour its time, and her irony was always brisker than it was deep. What she loved above all was *fun*—the farce of life in its wildest and subtlest surprises; and how wild they could be, and how subtle, how blandly disguised, there was none like her to discover. Her eye flew to the two ends of a paradox, floating innocently side by side, and pounced upon the rich nonsense they engendered as they joined. That was sport royal—I don't think there was any she liked better; and her laughter as she leads it comes ringing out of the shades. Anyone who crossed looks with her at the right moment will always remember it.

'The first time I met her,' writes Lady Aberconway
—and I must mention that this was actually a meeting of
much later years, but its place is perfect here—

was at a dinner to which John Hugh-Smith had
invited me, saying: 'I want you to meet Edith
Wharton; you will find her very intelligent'—and
then unfortunately for my peace of mind he had
added, 'but she doesn't really care for women.'

On arriving at his flat that evening I realised
that Mrs. Wharton and myself were the only women
present; it was to be a party of four. I arrived a little
late—or didn't I?—she may have been staying in
John's flat. Anyhow she was there when I arrived.
As I came into the room I saw an elderly woman,
very well dressed, with a black velvet ribbon round
her neck, whose face, I thought, was unusually
square and impassive. We were introduced, I
suppose we shook hands; all I remember is that she
then continued talking to the third guest, while I
observed her more closely.

For some reason that black velvet band round
her neck made her look rather formidable. I began
to anticipate with some dismay those inevitable
moments later in the evening when she and I would
be left to entertain each other. Her dress, I then
noticed, was quite perfect: black satin—elegant
yet suitable. But the black velvet ribbon at the base
of her neck continued to disconcert me. Then my
eyes wandered downwards and I looked at her feet.
What entrancing shoes she was wearing, exquisitely cut, with large sparkling buckles. And they
covered such *very* pretty feet.

And then I became aware that the feet were jutting out just a little further than was necessary from beneath the hem of her dress.

I took courage. The black velvet band was no longer so intimidating; the shoes delighted me.

I fancy that I can fix the exact moment when she first really liked me. It was during dinner that evening when something I said amused her. She looked up at me across the table and laughed, and as I looked back at her I realised that we could be friends, and I realised too how much I wanted her friendship.

Would it amuse you to hear the story that amused her? She and John had been discussing the quality of curiosity, and, rather tentatively, I had intervened, saying that the most inquisitive human being I knew was a certain friend of us all. Then I went on to describe how, at a luncheon-party, during a lull in the conversation, I had overheard him saying to a clergyman's wife, 'What!—you have been *three* times round the world and have only *one* child?!!' I can recall her chuckle as she agreed that only someone with the true gift of curiosity could have uttered that comment.

Later, after dinner, when we were alone, she suggested that she was probably the feminine counterpart of our friend, for she confessed to being deeply curious. I countered by saying that Virginia Woolf had a far greater curiosity, a mind that really delighted in hearing the most surprising and unlikely facts—to which, I added, she invariably gave a sort of symbolic twist peculiarly her own.

Edith didn't quite like that. Had Virginia really a great curiosity, she queried: certainly a very imaginative mind, perhaps a very poetic mind— but was she fundamentally endowed with *true* curiosity? And then, her own curiosity urging her on, she questioned me about my children, asking what it was like to *talk* to a child, to talk often, indeed every day, to a really *young* child.

If I had kept a diary I fancy I should have written in it that night: 'Dined with John Hugh-Smith to meet Mrs. Wharton. Her curiosity about things and people exceeds even Virginia's. She stimulates everyone. I want her for my friend.'

VI

53 Rue de Varenne

The charming apartment in the Rue de Varenne is now to be seen in a new light. It has already been visited when it was thronged with company—with Edith in the midst, working and even overworking for their enjoyment and her own; and now we behold it in a quiet hour, with nobody there but she and one other, seated on either side of the fireplace in the *petit salon,* small but fit. It is true that even in such an hour the room, rather crowded with fine furniture, was not a place to sprawl or lounge in; but the proliferation of new books on the tables, wherever they could be piled or ranked, eased its manner; the shaded lamps were friendly, the fire crackled on the swept hearth, and it was strange to think that Paris was muffled in the provincial hush without. Edith sat in her *bergère,* not as upright as usual; for when she was freely interested her shoulders sank, her eyes warmed, her face relaxed, and she seemed to shake off and push aside everything that didn't matter as she reached forward to the subject of the talk. It was thus that she talked of books—of books from the inside, books as they are brought into being, books as they press the writer closing with their demands: books as they stand up and take the light, dropping the writer,

53 RUE DE VARENNE

in their achieved independence. Into such talk she sub-
sided like a homing bird. Her hands were idle and empty,
save for the gold-handled eyeglass that was always ready
to flirt open for the page to be read, the illustration to
be sought, as one point led to another; for when she
had a friend with her as deeply concerned as herself
in these affairs there was no end to the pursuit. What an
example she was, an artist of such accomplishment, an
enquirer so impassioned, a student so absorbed!—and
here at last she sat in peace and talked at leisure with
this other enquirer, now her friend.

It seemed, with the passing days, a fortress of beauty
and security to be lodged in, as the guest surrendered
to the calm attention of the household, the soundless
regularity of the ministrations to his ease. In those early
morning hours of Edith's seclusion over her story—not
so closely sealed but that a gay little note, thrown off
as it were between chapters, would appear for the
guest on his breakfast-tray, with a greeting and a plan
for the day—here in these hours was a choice opportunity for him to do beautiful work of his own, in such
a fostering atmosphere: in this exquisite little study, for
example, overlooking the quiet *cité*, where the writing-
table is stocked (as we heard before) with everything
imaginable to tempt a writer's hand—if that could fire
his brain. Somehow, between observing it all and enjoying it carefully, which takes time, the work waits and
the hours pass; there is so much to distinguish, so much
of which it is desirable to be exactly conscious before
you begin; and behold it is time for the little plan projected, the morning walk that she never liked to miss.
Off we go, briskly stepping out through the cool grey
streets, away to the river, the bridge—to that other Paris

which seems, after our careless London, to tick and click so neatly in the clockwork of its morning industry. No aimless loitering for anybody and certainly not for us; it is a precise round that we follow, with an errand to be accomplished in its place. The errand, I must say, was apt to prove, without warning, to be Edith's appointment with her tailor or her dentist, and you find yourself suddenly left in a doorway for an unspecified term; these people who live by the clock keep time for themselves, and when the companion drops out of the *horaire* he must hang in suspense till it includes him again. I think we most of us remember that we have waited for Edith in a good many doorways—till she reappears, without explanation or embarrassing apology, and we resume the time-table together and trip home to lunch. There is just time for her to change whatever had to be changed in her apparel (she was always changing—her things never seemed suitable for two consecutive occasions) before lunch is announced. 'I must warn you,' Henry James had said to me, in thoughtful reminiscence, on the eve of my first visit to the Rue de Varenne, 'against the constant succession, in our dear Edith's hospitality, of succulent and corrupting meals.' They were his words, and I couldn't improve them.

We were alone when we talked about books; but there was another inmate in the house, who had slipped noiselessly out of the room when we fell to our discussion. This was Anna Bahlmann, her good governess of old days, now installed in the Rue de Varenne as secretary, treasurer, companion—I don't know what, but the title was of no consequence. She was American, of German parentage, and she was very small and unobtrusive, but quite a little personage too, with a droll little humour behind her spectacles, a wild little bravery beneath her gentility—a trifle astray in her surroundings, yet mistress of them in her degree. Only one anxiety confessedly tormented her: what could Edith give her to do, couldn't she give her more to do, to justify her position? Edith was full of understanding of such scruples. It mattered not at all to her what Anna did or didn't do, so that Anna was happy and provided for in her years; but she quite knew that it mattered much to Anna, and she was ingenious and imaginative in protecting her feelings. One good way would be to place her in control of the household expenditure; but this was soon defeated by Anna herself. 'When I see, my dear,' said she, desperately, 'what your expenses are, and the many calls on you, it is quite impossible for me to add to them by taking a salary.' It mattered little to Edith, I dare say, what Anna took or didn't take; but things must be adjusted to suit her compunction, so I suppose she was relieved of the eye-opening, breath-taking accounts. Perhaps she found her peace in typing the morning chapters. It was altogether a charming and amusing relation: Edith protective, indulgent, considerate, the ardent young pupil become the bountiful guardian-angel; and Anna the governess, proud of the transfiguration of her young charge, tenderly attached and devoted, but preserving her upright little independence in the midst of all this exotic glory. She slipped in and out of the company as she chose, with perfect discretion, for a few years, till she slipped out of the world. A quaint, pleasing, most individual little memory.

A weightier presence was in the background, that of the English butler, White—a kindly master, with very distinct views as to the manner in which Edith should

be served and her establishment ordered. They were old
friends of many years; they had studied their art and
matured in it together, so she always said; but one felt
that it was he who watched over her progress and had
seen to it that she never swerved from the perfect way.
He served her, as G. L. put it, with respectful severity;
and she very well knew she could rely on him, not only
to keep her taste true to the highest mark, but to safe-
guard and help her, to lift trouble off her back, in every
way that appertained to his department and I don't
know in how many more. And another presence too was
in the background, or rather everywhere, at any rate
wherever in her fondness and solicitude she could occupy herself for the care of Edith—her watchfully assiduous, dauntlessly tenacious Alsatian maid, with her
wise old puckered face and crumpled smile. Gross's eye
and hand were all-searching; and if there was nothing
else to be done for the moment she could peep in unseen upon the company and measure its effect, fine as it
might be, suitable company for her Edith; but having appraised it shrewdly, 'personne n'était si bien que
Madame' would be her satisfied report. Gross and Edith,
their alliance also had been long and close, and nothing
was pleasanter to see than their meeting again after
any separation. For as time went on Gross was persuaded to delegate her more fatiguing duties to others,
at least to another of whom even she could approve as a
companion to Edith on her travels; and when they met
again (after copious correspondence in the interval),
there was Edith greeting and embracing Gross, laughing
and chattering to her, excited and delighted as a small
girl home for the holidays. So Gross and White in partnership mounted guard over her and accepted her friends

as their own, which they all became. White was on the watch to the end, and as much as ever, or more than ever, when he had retired from active service, to remain ever loyally at hand. Gross, poor little old Gross, drooped at last in illness and her mind wandered—but all that was far in the future in these Parisian days, when Gross and White were in the strength of their trusted watch and ward.

There was also Cook—behind whose massive back we were seated for the afternoon drive. The drive was like the walk, no aimless outing; it was an excursion of shapely design, embracing an interesting object. But nothing was more difficult to Edith than to sit submissive and inactive behind her driver; it was an abdication in the conduct of her affairs that seemed always unnatural. The wheel must be left to Cook; but whether the way was the right way, the turn the wrong turning— whether the motor wasn't behaving oddly and what was the meaning of its complaints—who had mislaid the map and whether it was rightly interpreted when found: by many such distracting queries she made up for her exclusion from the helm. Cook, grandly calm, letting out the few words of his New England speech from a corner of his twisted mouth, pacified her fears with the assurance of knowledge and the ease of long habit; there was nothing to be done with Cook but to trust him where he presided. Cook surveyed the world, over so much of which he was projected in her service, with the good-humoured composure and impartiality with which he received her anxieties. Nothing shook his monumental breadth; unknown tongues, strange manners and unhomely customs beat on it in vain. He breasted the stream of Paris as it might have been a clatter of chil-

dren at play, and we slid off to the Bois, to the great
bends of the river, to the green country. In Edith's company, wherever she might be, there was always a perpetual radiation of trips, small voyages of discovery,
explorations near and far; but life in Paris was naturally
less centrifugal than elsewhere, and from St. Cloud
or St. Germain, with one swift impression of beauty and
interest, or two if there is time, we swing round towards
home: still with many tempting plans of larger scope ever
in the air, to be realised how or when?—we never know,
or we only know that we must leave them all to Edith,
to her hour and power. She is providence, not to be
pressed or forced, but to be waited on; the hour comes
to those who will wait. I advise a complete suspension of
particular hopes or wishes; don't set your mind on this
or that, but take what comes—much will come in any
case, as you will discover before long. Cook drew up at
the door in the Rue de Varenne just in time for her to
change for tea.

Who shall drop in to tea on a winter's evening, when
the curtains are drawn and the silence of the Faubourg
isolates us again in our fortress? This is not the moment
for the sort of assembly of which we heard before; this
is the time for a friend or two of the inner circle, always
free of the house: a circle naturally small, but it was also
elastic—French chiefly, and then chiefly American, and
English as might happen. Their faces are familiar, their
voices speak as I listen; I should know that voice anywhere, with its comfortable splutter and chuckle, and
that with its low penetrating comment, and that with its
suave authority; and how easily I see that face of clever
experience, that of fine young intelligence, that of rare
and gleaming beauty: men and women, older and

younger, mostly younger and mostly men. These are not here to be named or portrayed—or only one, whom I put aside but for a moment; they are to be sought, and most of them I think to be found, in her own record of memory. I don't know why they were all of the inner circle—who ever does? But there they were, and Edith, when she accepted a familiar companion, accepted that one thoroughly, and didn't cast about to remember what he hadn't to give. At any rate he wouldn't be there, I safely generalise, if he hadn't two things to offer—that which answered her humanity and that which met the precision of her mind. Don't be treacherous, do be reasonable: these were her absolute injunctions, not with impunity to be infringed. She, so trenchant in judgment, might occasionally surprise by her tolerance, but never by any accommodation with the spirit that is false to life. She drew away from it wherever it appeared, with whatever arts disguised—not without leaving her disapproval to be seen and felt. I like to insist on this, so clearly it comes back to me that the temper of the talk where she ruled it, as sharp-spoken as you please, was always one that nourished and expanded life, never one that blighted or exhausted it. Mock the world if you will, sting it if you can, bless it if you dare—but in any case don't make dust of it, don't drain it of its vital juices: that was her ordinance, and there was no leakage of colour and value in the world, though there might be plenty of broken heads, when she and her friends had said their say. The other injunction held no less; wilful and wayward unreason, however appealing, had the shortest of shrifts.

Apart from the rest, in a place by himself, and at the same time closely united with them all, most constant and most welcome—here is the friend whom I name for his own sake, and also for a new reason that now constrains me. Him indeed it would be impossible to omit, for there was that in Charles Du Bos which absolutely forbids, in any friend of his, any appearance of indifference when he approaches. There could only be instant response to one who came to meet you so trustfully, so winningly, so thoughtfully, offering all the great gifts of his intelligence and his sensibility without the shade of a reserve. He offered them to you, so to speak, for your own, as though his interest in them was their power, if it might be, to make a way into your friendship; and all the resources of his patient reflection were yours, for community and mutual understanding. I never knew anyone so free from any line of defence about himself; there was no enclosure of his mind, no barrier or warning sign; and original as it was, and marked all through with his own deliberate gravity and grace, enriched by his own warm candour, his mind was never a retreat for himself, but always a place of meeting and communication with the friend whose intimacy was to be won. The perfect simplicity and fearlessness of his advance, with all the elaboration of his mental and spiritual scruples, all the refinement of his civilisation— and the sweetness of the temper and character behind it, unsuspicious as a child, with all the enlightenment of his earnest veracity: these are memories to make one feel that a careless or thoughtless word must never be breathed, of all the world, to Charlie. Who ever dreamed of such a thing? Nobody knew him who could think of him but with a peculiar kindness and fondness first, before any other thought of the rare endowment of his nature. One of the finest and subtlest intelligences of his generation, and a charming serious child, breaking into his slow smile to greet you with confiding friendliness: this is Charles Du Bos, of whom I can write as I do because he has left us but a few days before these words are written.

When I see Edith and Charlie together—as I did so often, for his friendship was to her as to others a special possession, sometimes with indulgence and laughter, always with consideration and care to be cherished—when I see them together I can't help remarking at once how much she brought with her that to him meant nothing at all. There was something more than childlike, something angelic about Charlie that closed his eyes completely to many mortal preoccupations—though there were some of the practical order that he was forced, as an honest angel domiciled among men, to take in reckoning, and these cost him many anxious thoughts and painful decisions. But save where they actually impinged they did not exist for him; the world of which Edith was so conscious was for Charlie out of sight and out of hearing. He lived and moved in it indeed: what else, with his absorption in the spirit of man, could he do?—he could only exist where he was in communication with other minds; but he moved in a world that was exquisitely invisible, transparently immaterial, for all the warmth of its humanity. To penetrate and divine the souls of the elect—that was his work and joy; and in his fine angelic humility he was ready to presume the election of any soul that he encountered, and to question and explore it till at last it justified his belief—sometimes, I can well imagine, to its own surprise. But how could he deal with Edith—elect, no doubt, but so very much at home in the world, at once

so much in command of it and so defended against it—
the world that was nothing to him? He will presently
speak about this, and we shall understand the slightly
perplexed and puzzled tone of his conclusion. How is it
possible, he seemed to ask, that people should not be all
of a piece, consistent through and through? It was impossible for him to be anything else, and his persevering
efforts to find consistency in others have reminded me
of the attempts of the old astronomers to make order of
the observed movements of the heavenly bodies. All
would be easy but for those straying planets, disturbing
the celestial march, that require the building of so in-
tricate a system, 'cycle and epicycle, orb in orb,' before
they will consent to be resolved into an universal harmony. The system grew so top-heavy that it all but tot-
tered. And then came Edith and swept it away with her
summary stroke of laughter and realism; and Charlie
smiled, but without conviction, and set to work again
from the beginning.

Indeed it never seemed as though our world could
be his home, or the right place for his habitation. He
must be disappointed in the end; we should never be all
that he desired and deserved to find us. In one way only
the world could make it up to him—with its affection;
and certainly in that way it did its best, and he returned
it with his self-forgetful fidelity. He was happy in friendship, more so in nearer ties; he was happy in his wish
to admire, his inclination to revere, his need to worship.
The time came later when he discovered a haven in
which, as I suppose, wish and need were finally satisfied—the haven of the Catholic faith; but of this I cannot speak. For my part, looking back, though I see him
always in sociable converse, yet I see him solitary, never

really among his kind, for there were no others of his kind thus domiciled among men. He was happiest, one might think, with the great spirits of the dead, and there most fitly received: not with the great dead as they were in life, for they too were men, but with their memory that survives, bearing their sheaves. These he could encircle with his sensitive and prehensile imagination to his heart's content; it was in the stillness of the past that there was time for greatness and beauty to answer the questions of this spirit athirst for communion. He lost that baffled look in the company of genius dead and gone, where he could range at leisure, moving unhurried from one great name to another—pausing and settling before each in turn, in the stations of his pilgrimage, to offer the tribute of his finest appreciation. Life harassed him as it could, and indeed it could too well, so care-ridden, so conscientious as he was; but the youth of his enthusiasm in the eventful journey of his thought, this was fresh to the end—the end that came to it the other day. He died in August, 1939, aged fifty-seven. He had sent me, not long before, some pages written for this book. By all who knew him his voice, speaking of his friend, will be recognised with fond remembrance.

VII

A letter from Charles Du Bos

For some two years before his death Charles Du Bos had been settled in America, as Assistant Professor of English at the University of Notre Dame in Indiana; and it was from there that he wrote to me about Edith Wharton. (He wrote in English—he was himself English by his mother's side and used his two languages at will, speaking or writing; and if in English he seemed at times to exhaust the power of words to follow his thought, I should say he did the same in French—French that was native to him and intimate with him as English could hardly be.) He wrote, then, on my appeal, from his university of the Middle West, in the face of many difficulties; for he was very closely occupied with his duties, and hampered also, as he too often was, by ill-health. It was in the form of a letter to me that he preferred to write, a letter in which he could speak at ease of his long association with our friend. He was at this time planning to write a book (I believe he had already given lectures) on her work as a novelist, and it will be seen how her work had acquired in his thought a particular significance in her life. If he strained the meaning of it in some directions, as I think he did, it was from a very characteristic desire to recover in her work, or her relation to it, that which he missed (nor he alone) in her commerce with her friends—that unreserved freedom, as natural in him as breathing, which to her was so difficult and strange. For such a woman to be shy of life, even of life friendly and responding, should mean and must mean that she found perfect liberation elsewhere, and he found it for her. I am not sure of his reading of her art, nor convinced that she was other with her books than she was with her friends. But here at any rate is a view of Edith Wharton that in a very special manner is also a view of Charles Du Bos, and they are seen in each other's company with living truth. This is the 'letter' that he sent me:

'The soul of the novel, which is (or should be) the writer's own soul.' You remember Edith's memorable pronouncement—a pronouncement which, beyond the novel as such, traces the mysterious line of demarcation that in every kind of writing separates major from minor work, however perfectly executed. With her it was never a case of the *should be:* her soul always *was* the soul of all her writing. In another passage of *A Backward Glance* she speaks of her 'discovery of that soul of mine which the publication of my first volume called to life.' She has never said anything truer of herself, anything that introduces us more directly into the centre. In Edith soul and work are interdependent, and that is why in her books she gives herself wholly—though of course only to readers who know how to read, and in the world of to-day, a world in itself unreadable, few such readers seem to subsist. But Edith's work is not the theme of this

[93]

memorial book, the book which you have planned. What you ask from each of us is the material out of which you will disengage her portrait as she was to her friends, as she appeared to them; and, as I have already told you, it is here, precisely here, that my personal difficulty lies. In *A Backward Glance* Edith did me the honour of calling me one of her 'closest friends,' and so I was, and for more than thirty years. There is no kindness that I did not experience at her hands, no literary or intellectual stimulus that I did not derive from her talk; and yet only once in our exchange did we reach out to what I at least consider as the test of complete intimacy—only once (to use the word that was applied to Thomas Gray) did she *speak out* to me. Now (and here again I must add, for me at least) all recollections that do not spring out of a fund of complete intimacy possess at the best but a secondary value. Nevertheless I cannot remain deaf to your appeal. The only time that I saw Henry James *en tête à tête*—he was staying with Edith in Paris—I asked him if he did not suffer too much from the overcrowded Parisian life he was then leading, and he answered, 'If every day I have but one hour to squeeze the sponge of the past, I am content.' I have tried for your benefit to squeeze the little sponge of my past, and I send you the few drops for whatever they may be worth.

Rue Barbet de Jouy: you have not forgotten that quiet street of the Faubourg St. Germain, so apart, yet, on account of the gardens of the Hotel Biron and the Hotel Chanaleillhes, not shut in, semi-rustic in its dignity; nor have you forgotten either, on the second floor of number 20, the drawing-room of the Paul Bourgets: the worn Maple furniture, upon which years had conferred a little of the style of the English eighteenth century, the silver Leuchars vases, and on the walls the few beautiful Sienese pictures, which our friend Berenson has not disdained to include in his catalogue: above all, the priceless Neroccio, the Madonna with James and Dominic, that hung on the mirror above the mantelpiece, the face of the Madonna, as so often with Neroccio, a mild, self-contained, yet piercing jewel. But Neroccio's was not the only madonna in the room. Under the protection of her wings, noiselessly, almost timorously, another madonna, with wings too, 'folded but never quiet,' lived there her life, the one which, with the tenderest care, Edith has preserved, embalmed for all who loved her. 'I shall never forget Minnie Bourget as I first saw her, with her little aquiline nose, her grave remote grey eyes and sensitive mouth, in the delicate oval of a small face crowned by heavy braids of brown hair. I used to call her the "Tanagra Madonna," so curiously did that little head combine the gravity of a mediaeval Virgin with the miniature elegance of a Greek figurine. Everything about her was shy, elusive and somehow personal to herself. . . . But I find no words delicate and imponderable enough to describe the Psyche-like tremor of those folded but never quiet wings of hers.' *

At the end of a November afternoon of 1905—I was then a youth of twenty-three—I was sitting

* *A Backward Glance*, p. 103.

alone with Minnie in the drawing-room and she
said to me, 'I have just finished reading a novel by
one of my best friends, Mrs. Wharton, an American.' She spoke of their meeting at Newport, of their
travels with the Whartons in Italy, of *The Valley
of Decision,* and then added, 'But this book, *The
House of Mirth,* is Edith Wharton's first great
modern novel, and I cannot say how impressed I
am by it. Take it with you; I am sure you will like it.'
I am not generally, like Edith's Justine, 'a flame-
like devourer of the page,' far rather, like her Am-
herst 'a slow absorber of its essence'; yet of Edith's
books—and in the process of re-reading no less that
in that of reading (and how often have I not re-
read all her books!)—I have always been the flame-
like devourer. I devoured *The House of Mirth* on
the spot, and there and then, before having met her,
my intimacy with Edith began. At that first stage
of my literary apprenticeship Bourget was my
'great task-master,' and, as in the Miltonic sonnet,
I was ever living in his eye. A stern task-master he
was, but I was then a bundle of hesitations, and he
was legitimately exasperated in the presence of
what he called, after Benjamin Constant, my *démon
de la procrastination.* As I was imprudent enough
to mention to him, no less than to Minnie, my un-
bounded admiration for *The House of Mirth,* he
decided, with the irresistible authority which never
forsook him, that I was to translate the book, and
that by trying my hand at it I should at least prove
whether or not I *had* a hand. And so it was, when
a few weeks later the Whartons arrived in Paris,

that I was presented to Edith as the eventual translator of her first masterpiece.

For the youth that I then was the predicament was a rather formidable one, and in our first encounters it did not lead on my part to ease of intercourse: the less so that I had not then the slightest idea that Edith was *shy*—that shyness to which she herself alludes more than once in *A Backward Glance*, which I was to identify soon after, which remained in her such an inveterate trait, and which constitutes the key to all her social demeanour outside the circle of close friendship. Besides I was not then sufficiently versed in psychology to know that personal shyness may coexist with the swift and unfailing sureness of step that I so admired in *The House of Mirth*. The result was that, though by no means a shy person myself, I felt shy at first with Edith, attributing what in her was shyness to a sureness of step precisely that I was unable to emulate. In talk Edith always considered the interlocutor her equal. It was the finest characteristic of her wholly civilised politeness, but on that very account she postulated in me a range of culture which I did not possess, and I often missed the point by her rich play of allusions. Nevertheless, for the literary apprentice, to drop in at tea-time at the Hotel Dominici, to listen to talk even but half apprehended, to think of Lily Bart (with whom I was a little in love)—all this had the flavour of a *romanesque* adventure. Bourget always called Edith *le Velásquez*, and the name suited her high restraint, that quality of the subdued everywhere

[97]

present in her and around her, a quality which had nothing of the Whistlerian deliberateness, but which was a native grace akin to that of the master of *Las Meninas.* It must have been about the same time that Bourget wrote a short *nouvelle,* of which the title now escapes me—you must remember that I am writing here far from all my books: the *nouvelle* was not much, but Bourget himself told me that he had thought of Edith in writing it: it bore upon the relation of a rich American woman with her maid, who had become the accomplice of a robbery at her expense, and it had at least the merit of bringing out most accurately that side of Edith's character which struck all who knew her—her inexhaustible and delicate kindness, understanding, pity and mercy for those who were in any way dependent upon her.

And this is the moment to answer your question as to what Edith *was* for Bourget. As is shown by his masterpiece, the *Essais de Psychologie Contemporaine,* Bourget's attitude towards his elders, and no less when they were still alive than when they were already dead, was always the most sterling trait of his nature, the one trait in fact which amounted to a kind of genius, not only in his critical writings but still more in his conversation, which (I agree with Edith) was among the best I ever heard. But, except in the case of Barrès (and even then only of the young Barrès, for the greater Barrès he was never able quite to appreciate), his attitude towards his contemporaries and the writers of the following generations was quite the reverse: not owing to any mean motive—he was incapable of that—but owing to an overweight of authority that reacted upon himself no less irresistibly than upon others. I once applied to him in my essay upon his critical work (and he had the liberality not to resent it) Joubert's profound saying on Bonald: *'Il se trompe avec une force!'* Here you have the whole matter in a nutshell, the explanation of why Bourget was always sure that he was right. In the case of Edith, however, we meet with the exception that proves the rule. Bourget admired Edith's personality, and he admired her all the more because, scarcely less than Carlyle, he was the preacher of the 'gospel of work.' That a wealthy *femme du monde* should work, work seriously, attach such importance to all questions of *métier*, have a literary conscience—this was the object not only of his admiration but of his approval, and Bourget could only admire wholeheartedly when he could approve.

As Edith says in *A Backward Glance*, it was in the course of our work on *The House of Mirth* that I became one of her closest friends. Meanwhile, in 1907, I had married. Between Edith and my wife a friendship sprang up immediately that for thirty years, until Edith's death, never knew a shadow, and thus my marriage strengthened also my personal link with Edith herself. In that same year, 1907, Edith was at the beginning of those thirteen years of Paris life which were spent entirely in the Rue de Varenne, and of which she says: 'All those years rise up to meet me whenever I turn the corner of the street.' First number 58, the apartment twice sublet to her by the George Vanderbilts in that stately Louis XIV *hôtel:* then number 53, with the outlook on the Cité de Varenne, harbour of aristocratic seclusion, the ideal setting for *The American* of Henry James, constituting in itself one of those 'synthetic' photographs that he devised for the New York edition of his novels and tales. *La douceur de vivre:* which of us does not apply Talleyrand's saying to those last pre-war years?—and I for one with a difference, persuaded that the end of the *ancien régime* offered no treasures comparable to the Isadora Duncan of 1909–10, to the Russian Ballet, to the first reading of Proust's *Du côté de chez Swann*. In those seven years hardly a week elapsed without exchanges between the Rue de Varenne and the Rue de la Tour. Exchange is the right word, especially if applied to the exchange of friends: to Edith we owe you, we owe Gaillard Lapsley, many others now 'all gone into the world of light,' and to us Edith owed not a few of her French friends.

The other great exchange was, of course, talk—talk that was an exchange precisely because, on the footing of equality that was so dear to Edith, each interlocutor was invited both to speak and to listen, the very opposite of the cage of parrots which, on the eve of his death, in a letter to his cousin Rosalie, Benjamin Constant so aptly characterises: *'Je suis las de vivre dans un monde où tout le monde parle et où personne n'écoute.'* Culture and Anarchy: it was you who many years ago, in Edith's garden of the Pavillon Colombe, commended Matthew Arnold's book to me, and perhaps the title of the book, better than anything else, defines the kind and quality of her talk. Rather than creative, inspired or inspiring, her talk had the value and virtues of the very utterance of culture. Everything and everybody was placed by her where it should be placed, related to the never disturbed and never forgotten background of the great traditional references; and in that respect nothing is more self-revealing than the admirable sentence of Traherne that she chose as a motto for *The Writing of Fiction*, 'Order the beauty even of Beauty is.' Anarchy under any form, but most of all anarchy of judgment, was abhorrent to her. Yet, for the incurable improviser and lover of uniqueness (as distinguished from *relatedness*) that I am, there was at times something forbidding, almost chilling, in the degree of her mental equipoise. With the sole exception of the craft or writing of fiction—in the discussion of which she always gave herself all leisure, because the theme was to her of inexhaustible significance—Edith's *tempo* in talk was a *scherzo*, and even a *scherzo* in *pizzicato*. Every topic that arose was by her too swiftly shelved. She never seemed to enjoy immersion for immersion's sake, which to me is the condition and also the atmosphere of the most satisfactory kind of talk. Perhaps there is a contradiction between skating and taking the plunge—and Edith was such a flawless skater. In talk a certain impatience made her averse to concentrating, and in *A Backward Glance* she herself admits the fact: 'I never learned to concentrate except on subjects naturally interesting to me, and developed a restless curiosity which prevented my fixing my thoughts for long even on these.'

But, as I said in the beginning, she did once *speak out* to me, and that happened in 1912, a year which turned out to be in every way the *annus mirabilis* of our intimacy. To lead up to what then took place, I am obliged to enter for a moment into my personal history. 1912 was for me the year of a double discovery—the discovery of the novels of George Eliot and of the love-poems of Browning. In the sense in which a novel can be a whole world, a world in itself, for me the discovery of George Eliot was second in importance only to that of Tolstoi. Edith and I had one trait in common, a total imperviousness and what I make bold to call a healthy contempt for any manifestation of the *Zeitgeist*, and we laughed away the idea of considering George Eliot from a Victorian or anti-Victorian angle. I never met anybody who understood George Eliot better or admired her more than Edith, and now that she is no longer with us I mostly keep the subject to myself. I remember her reading to me, in *The Mill on the Floss*, the two passages on the beauty of Maggie's arm, adding, 'To think that there are fools who pretend that there is no physical life, no sensuousness in George Eliot!' For us both *Middlemarch* was of course the greatest achievement of all—the book of which, after the anti-Victorian wave had spent itself, Virginia Woolf was to say, 'It is one of the few English novels written for adults.' We always came back to *Middlemarch*, and in the Dorothea-Ladislaw scenes Edith used to compare the presence of Will in the room to the presence of a portrait by Titian. As for Browning's love-poems, 'Prospice' was my first

[102]

initiation, but even this, the greatest poem of love
beyond death, had to yield to 'By the Fireside,' the
greatest poem of love in life, in married life; whilst
Edith put above all others 'Any Wife to Any Husband,' to which she had recently introduced us.

Such was the situation on that day of August,
1912, when Edith came to lunch at the country-
home of my in-laws at La Celle Saint-Cloud. My
wife was ill in bed, and after Edith had seen her she
carried me off in her motor to show me the church
of Montfort l'Amaury. The church we did in fact
visit, but to me it is as if I never saw it, so absorbed,
so impressed was I by what had occurred during
the drive. I had quoted as contradictory in appearance, as complementary in reality, the words
of Dorothea to Rosamond: 'Marriage is so unlike
anything else—there is something even awful in
the nearness it brings,' and the lines in 'By the Fireside,'

> Oh, the little more, and how much it is!
> And the little less, and what worlds away!

and it was then that Edith *spoke out:* 'Ah, the
poverty, the miserable poverty, of any love that lies
outside of marriage, of any love that is not a living
together, a sharing of all!' In the wonderful last
scene between Selden and Lily you remember the
sentence, 'He felt it only as one of those rare moments which lift the veil from their faces as they
pass.' Such a moment was the one we were living;
we remained silent, but it was the silence of utter
communing; for once the angel of intimacy had
spread its wings over us.

Two months later Edith lent me the proofs of *The Reef*. After reading them I told Edith that by the small number of protagonists, the architectural economy of proportions, the passionate poignancy enhanced by the exquisite restraint of expression, no novel came closer to the quality of a tragedy of Racine. At our following meeting Edith showed me a letter she had just received from Henry James, the letter on *The Reef* written at Lamb House on December 4, 1912, which in 1920, thanks to your editorship of his letters, was to be enshrined in the *thesaurus* of which it constitutes one of the chief glories. Towards any critical judgment of Henry James I stood (and in many ways I still stand) in a state of abjection—the word being taken exactly in the sense in which Henry James himself so often took it. Having said that, it is useless to describe what was my feeling when I came upon the passage: 'The beauty of it is that it is, for all it is worth, a Drama, and almost, as it seems to me, of the psychologic Racinian unity, intensity and gracility. Anna is really of Racine, and one presently begins to feel her throughout as an Eriphyle or a Bérénice.' That Henry James should have happened to intervene thus in function of *The Reef* and Racine at the end of 1912, gave for me the finishing touch, the unhoped-for and totally unexpected crowning to the *annus mirabilis* of our intimacy.

But, as Edith wrote, rare are those moments, and in the twenty-five years that followed no other such moment was to occur. I seem to touch here the fundamental difference in our natures. To me

that moment of complete outspokenness and the
utter communing to which it had given rise appeared as a beginning, a beginning of our intimacy;
and it was inevitable that to me it should appear
so because, not being shy, I have no difficulty in
speaking out. For Edith evidently it was quite the
reverse. I should not be sincere if I did not say
that I was disappointed, and seventeen years later
I ran the risk of reminding her of that intimate moment (though of course without alluding to what
had caused it) in the hope that our intimacy might
be renewed. But the attempt proved fruitless. It
happened thus. In my book on Byron, to illustrate
the feelings of Lady Byron when at last she is
obliged to become conscious of the relations between Byron and his half-sister, I had quoted
Edith's sentence on Anna: 'She felt as if her
thoughts would never again be pure'; and in the
dedication on the fly-leaf of the copy that in June,
1929, I brought to Edith, then our neighbour at the
Trianon Palace at Versailles, I referred, in terms of
the tenderest thanksgiving, to our intimate talk and
to all that it had meant for me. Was such a risk
considered by Edith as a challenge, perhaps an in-
discreet one? I do not know, I only know that she
never alluded to that dedication. I took her silence
as a final answer and never reopened the subject;
but the result of all this was that I cherished more
than ever the memory of our unique moment, and
to-day, whilst writing to you, it lives in me less as
a memory than as one of those steady lights which
are a solace when one friend more has gone. Having
said as much, it would be futile to enter into fur-

ther details of a friendship that continued unabated until the end. One fact only should be mentioned, because, beyond and above all personal ties, it bears upon Edith's boundless generosity. In October, 1914, when André Gide, myself and a few French and Belgian friends founded 'Le Foyer Franco-Belge,' a little war-work for the French and Belgian refugees, our resources were so insufficient that I turned to Edith for help. She immediately created the 'American Hostels,' which functioned as one with 'Le Foyer'; and all through the war, thanks to the liberal response of America and thanks to the invaluable co-operation of her friends, Royall and Elisina Tyler, she devoted a great part of her energies and of her time to the saving and tending of numberless French and Belgian refugees.

'As a Bérénice,' Henry James had said of Anna, and both Bérénice and Anna reappeared in our talk the last time I was to see Edith. It was in July, 1936. I was in bed in my home, Ile Saint-Louis, in the middle of a period of eighteen months' illness in bed. I was permitted to see one friend a day for a short time; but when Edith came, and as if I foresaw that it was to be our last meeting, though at that time it seemed more probable that I should be the first to depart, I refused to let her go. I was then reading the book of Maurice Levaillant that had just come out, *Chateaubriand, les Mémoires d'Outre-Tombe, et Madame Récamier*, and what a talk we had on Chateaubriand, Madame Récamier, Benjamin Constant and Madame de Staël. In the preceding days I had re-read both *Bérénice* and

The Reef. I had been struck more than ever by the
affinity of the two works, but also more than ever
had I felt a slight discrepancy in the last chapter of
The Reef, which, brilliant as it is in itself, belongs
to another vein of Edith's, the vein of *The Custom
of the Country,* and thereby, by a touch of bitterness, despoils the novel of the sweet yet majestic
sadness of the close of Racine's tragedy. I mentioned the fact to Edith; she agreed with the utmost
gentleness and seemed touched by my faithfulness
to that book of hers which had been the book of
our *annus mirabilis.* Thus, to use the saying of Mary
Stuart, our end was in our beginning.

I know not which of the two friends is to be seen
more clearly in the light of this sensitive retrospect:
Charlie, to whom the value of life was in certain rare
moments of illumination and nowhere else—or Edith,
to whom life was such an abundance of things, and its
reward in their variety; Charlie, unembarrassed and
demonstrative, unconscious of himself, eager to impart
and to share—or Edith, careful of her guard, mindful
of her privacy; and again Charlie, troubled in action,
hesitant and inexpert—and she so sure of her course
and of her will. I am not surprised that he, looking back,
should have dwelt with such intensity on that moment
of their long intercourse when her guard dropped, nor
yet that it was never followed by another; few of her
friends, perhaps, came nearer to her than that. Yet to
most of them, after all, this strict *clausura* of her choice,
so rarely broken, might seem more natural than it did
to him; it is not given to many to declare themselves
with his simplicity. Moreover, in the exchange of under-

[107]

standing between friend and friend, if the seal on speech is to be called shyness, it may also be called the desire to save a living thing from the pressure of words that limit it; and in Edith's reserve there was no constraint of sympathy and perception. She did not miss the intimacy that she seemed to refuse, for it was hers in a different way—not in words that were said, but through eyes that saw; and she was not afraid of being seen. Enough, this is a revealing chapter in the story of Edith Wharton among her friends, and no one could have written it but Charles Du Bos.

VIII

On the road

With the open road before her, dipping to some 'sparkling foreign country,' her heart leapt up—she was in her element; there was no such blithe or purposeful traveller as Edith when she set forth on one of her buc-caneering raids, with her cargo of books, her well-plotted itinerary, and a partner who shared her zeal without questioning her course. It must have been best of all in her early days, when she was still discovering, still rifling and amassing with both hands, and not a moment to lose if she was to carry home all that she desired and required. Long before the motor came to speed her passage she had possessed herself of wide lands and riddled their recesses—not the great places only of famed wealth, but the lanes and byways that lead to hidden rarities, lost treasures and forgotten shrines; she knew they were there, it was useless to tell her that they weren't or that she couldn't find them. She was not to be hindered, as those who would bar her progress quickly learn. Everyone yields to her firm and bland decision; or if not to that, then to the smart rate at which she is always prepared to pay her way (but within reason: what she called 'slopping money about' was an offence to her taste); or if ever that should fail, to the cutting flick of her command, which may take anyone aback. She rustled unhesitatingly into the locked church, the gallery that happened to be closed that day, the palace that wasn't shown to visitors: how well we know them, and how readily her companion would be content with the outside view! But it was ever advisable to follow the dauntless woman where she led; for as thorough as she was, she distinguished, she appraised, she spent no time where it was fruitless; and as earnest as she was, she never exhausted the charm of an adventure, she was always enjoying herself on a holiday. Nobody could ask for a better fellow-traveller on the road to El Dorado. It is true that the close of the day was wont to be stormy; you must reckon on a break in the weather when she views the provision that the roadside inn or the palatial hotel (it is all one) offers for her convenience. But it passes, and the sun is on the road again next morning.

El Dorado was mainly Italy for many years, as was only natural; but even in Italy she kept her head. She hadn't descended to the realms of gold to be carried away in a flood of romantic rapture, like other raiders from the north. When Henry James as a young man found himself for the first time in Rome he might have been seen, by his own account, wandering through the streets in a drunken ecstasy, reeling and moaning in a fever of delight; and he was not the last in the long succession of such revellers. But this was by no means the way of the young woman who followed him some dozen years or so later. I suppose there was then already a new spirit in the air, not less joyfully appreciative, but sharper in discernment; and the passionate pilgrim began to profit by the scholarship of fresh teachers, cooling his brow, quickening his vision. It was not for a bold young brain to submit for ever to Ruskin in his prophetic rage, veiling his gaze before the display of sinful pride in which the age of faith went down; nor even to desert Ruskin for Pater, throwing off moral bonds to be lost in a rainbow dream before the mysteries of pure art. Away with sentiment, anyhow: and behold at a stroke, so far from suffering a loss, how largely the treasury of Italy is enriched. Hadn't the pilgrim observed that of all which is before his eyes in Italy the greater part, indeed by far the greater, belongs to times and fashions that he had been schooled to ignore, or to notice only with scorn? What nonsense! If you love Italy as fervently as you profess, why turn your shoulder on so vast a portion of her genius? It was a new question—still too new for most of the fond devotees. Strange as it may seem in these days, there was originality and enterprise in Edith's determination to use her eyes as she chose; and it was like her spring-heeled love of action to seek the fields where there were new things to be said and done, instead of contentedly following the beaten paths. And the freshest field of all—where indeed hardly anyone was yet to be seen save one striking and redoubtable figure, Vernon Lee—was that Italy of the eighteenth century which was scarcely given a word, or but a word of disdain, in the doctrine that most of us were still imbibing at the end of the nineteenth. I remember my own surprise, early in the twentieth, when I opened a book called *Italian Backgrounds* and found that the author's idea of a background in Italy was what I had understood to be the most trivial of foregrounds, to be pushed through unremarked on the way to a nobler past. The more backward of us, at any rate, might begin to learn from Edith herself.

She was an intrepid teacher too. Not for her the diffidence, which may also be the slack timidity, of those who hold their tongues and reserve their judgment in provinces not their own. She hadn't rejected the sonorous prophet or the pale-mouthed priest to be over-awed by the specialist. * A person of culture, in the world that bred her youth, was not only allowed but expected to have the courage of his opinion in all the arts, and she had no idea of renouncing the privilege. She delivered her view with no misgiving or embarrass-ment; and her confidence may have betrayed her at times, but never in one matter, her quick recognition of the voice of real authority, wherever it spoke, and her prompt resort to its company. 'I have always,' so she put it, 'preferred the society of my betters'; and true enough her place in the schools of light and learning was by affinity with the masters—though not indeed at their feet: she sat with them at the high table, and talked and kept them talking. The learning that she tore from their books and their talk was not as thorough, I dare say, as her ease in drawing and announcing her conclusions; with her impatience, that was always plucking at her attention and rushing her pace, the mark of scholarship was not hers, nor likely to be; but even among the severest of the pundits her free ways, her refusal to be intimidated or talked down, might be found both whole-some and entertaining. Yet there was something else that she missed, not only accuracy in her studies. In her unwillingness to linger over an impression, to toy with it, to return to it, she often seemed to deny herself the reward of the amateur—the endless variety of his free-dom to take his pleasure as he finds it. She refused her

* I thank Sir Kenneth Clark for the suggestion here followed.

share of that long and dear adventure. G. L. reminds me of an apt little illustration. We were once at Bayeux on a summer afternoon, he and she and I; and though she gave us all the time we needed, he and I, for an examination of the famous 'tapestry,' as for herself she sat outside in the car while we went in to see it. She *had* seen it, she knew it, there was nothing more for her to do about it—why get out of the car to look at what she knew? The best of company in breaking new ground: but when it came to loitering in old haunts she began to fidget if you kept her waiting overlong.

It was best, once more, to take her hand and be guided by her. Here is now a pleasant glimpse of what might happen if you did—recalled by the same young English friend whom we saw, sometime ago, shyly calling on Mrs. Wharton in New York.

It was in 1903. My husband and I had snatched a fortnight in Florence from a dull winter of convalescence on the Riviera; and into our modest entresol overlooking Piazza Goldoni Edith flashed one April afternoon. We were engaged in planning our sightseeing in the town, but our visitor would have none of that. 'It's much too fine a day for galleries and churches—it's a day for the country and the villas. I'm going up to Fiesole, and you must come with me. You'll see a fine villa and a great ilex-wood—and Vernon Lee into the bargain.' This was an invitation not to be refused. I had longed for years to meet Vernon Lee, and I had not yet entered any of the famous villas over whose walls the wistaria and banksia roses tumbled so fragrantly. So off we went, all three of us, in the carriage that was waiting at the door, and all the way up the Fiesole hill Edith talked, gaily, learnedly, enchantingly. It appeared that she was planning a book on Italian villas and gardens, and must see all those in the neighbourhood of Florence before proceeding to the great palaces of the Milanese and the lakes. Not that there was very much to her purpose near Florence, the *giardino inglese*, with its lawns and winding paths and irregular flower-beds, having replaced all too many of the older formal gardens, with their careful plotting of sunshine and shade, their lemon-adorned terraces and economy of flowers. 'For flowers,' she explained, 'are not characteristic of Italian gardens. The old designers counted on permanent elements for their effects— vases and fountains and clipped ilexes and graded terraces.' All this was new to me, and I longed to hear more. And since to an eager enquirer Edith was always gracious, she willingly explained how some of the smaller towns, such as Siena and Lucca, owing to their poverty, had kept far more gardens of the old type, some deliciously rococo, others beautifully baroque. This last expression was too much for me. Beautifully baroque?—I had always understood that everything baroque was bad. 'Ah, you've been brought up on Ruskin,' she said, laughing outright. 'But I can't tell you now how wrong you are—we're nearly there.'

Indeed there was no more time for talk at that moment. We turned off the main road into a drive that led under rose-covered walls to the church-like façade and long loggia of La Doccia, where we were to drink tea. And there, beside our American

host, stood Vernon Lee herself, with her uncom-
promising mannish hat and dress, her strongly
marked features, and her witty, exciting, trenchant
speech. And for the next hour of enchantment I
could hardly spare attention for my tea or for the
most ordinary politeness to the kind man who was
plying me with American cakes and grapefruit (the
first I had ever seen), in my anxiety not to lose a
word of the best talk I had ever heard—Vernon
Lee's, most of it, but kept together and enlivened
by Edith's quick repartees and ringing laugh. I
thought it the most lovely place imaginable, and
that it would be perfect felicity to dwell in such
surroundings; and I little knew how near to that
spot, in another and more famous villa, I should
one day find my home.

As we drove down the hill in the sunset Edith
asked suddenly, 'What do you two serious young
people do when you are not in churches and picture-
galleries?' We said we had been going to some
lectures on Dante, in the hall of the Arte della
Lana, but found them rather dull. 'So I should
imagine,' she chuckled. 'Well, I went to them myself when I was your age. To-morrow you'll come
with me instead to some antiquity-shops. I'm trying to find some things for our new house—and it's
all part of your education.' I had been longing for
some guidance to the miscellaneous collections of
the shops in Via dei Fossi and Via Maggio, for I
myself was quite unable to distinguish good from
bad in such a medley, and my husband was not
interested in bric-à-brac. He was safely in the
Bargello when Edith appeared next morning, this

time with Mr. Wharton, and we three walked down the street, conveniently near, to Salvadori's. I saw at once that she held the key to the knowledge I wanted. Her eyes, bright and rapacious as a robin's, darted hither and thither over the ranks of carved and intarsia chests of drawers and writing-tables, cabinets filled with china and glass, walls covered with every variety of mirror. Then she pounced, it is the only word, on the object that attracted her. But if her movement was swift her eyes were no longer eager—cold and indifferent rather, as she pointed out the demerits of the pair of chests that I saw, and doubtless the dealer also saw, she meant to buy. Not, however, at the price he named—as to that she was quite clear, and she offered half. Slowly, patiently, disputing each point in the game, buyer and seller drew together, till the figure was reached which she, and possibly he too, had already decided upon. Mr. Wharton took in hand the rest of the business, and Edith passed on to glance, to pounce, to bargain again. By the end of the morning, in the various shops of the street, she had made half a dozen purchases, and I had had my first lesson in Italian shopping.

Other excursions followed these two—to villas, to shops, to the smaller and less-known churches of the city. But time was limited; both she and I were due at Salsomaggiore for the cure; and before the month was ended we had left the joys of Tuscany behind us and were settled in one of the few really ugly and uninteresting places in Italy. But even at Salso her high spirits did not fail. Our hotel, hideous, expensive and far from good, certainly aroused her ire; and we, who had been invited to sit at the Whartons' table, sometimes felt that we would rather have eaten a bad dinner, uninterrupted, than have seen so many dishes presented to us and whisked away, like Alice's leg of mutton, for some defect in the cooking or the service. She enjoyed badgering, I think, the haughty and saturnine manager—whom she nicknamed Twilight, from his habit of wearing a white evening tie with an afternoon coat, and who had never before had to change so many electric fittings, provide so many face-towels, or complain so often to the chef. But when the cat's-paw had passed she would be all laughter and talk again—though her husband would pass a hand rather wearily through his hair as he leant back after the conflict.

Only once did I get a glimpse of the fashionable New York lady who in Park Avenue had so disconcerted me. Mr. Wharton had preceded us after dinner to the hall, to order coffee and secure a comfortable corner, and when we followed we found him talking in the passage to two middle-aged ladies, clearly American. To my surprise Edith seemed not to perceive them, and she was passing without any sign of recognition when her husband called out, 'Oh, Pussy, don't you see the duchess?' Then indeed she did pause, gave a stiff bow in the direction of the group, and without further greeting proceeded, not to the hall but into the lift, beckoning to us to follow her. My husband did, but I lingered for a moment, desirous to see the end of the little scene. Mr. Wharton was all confused apology—that was easily seen. 'While she is taking

the cure my wife,' he said, 'has to rest a great deal—
she feels the cold too.' 'Yes,' said the duchess
serenely, 'I noticed the chill in the air.' Edith had
swept the scene, but the duchess had certainly
spoken the last word. In the Whartons' sitting-room
the air was still a little chilly. 'Those dreadful
women,' she said as her husband entered: 'we don't
see them at home—why should we here?' That was
all; and I had had a lesson, not my first, in the social
distinctions of New York.

The sight of that group on the terrace of La Doccia
carries me forward to a memory of my own—to an afternoon of another spring, some years later, in the setting
of one of those old gardens, near Siena, whose grave and
noble beauty had been saved by poverty and neglect. To
Edith, no doubt, it was long familiar; but this time there
was a firm hand on her sleeve, restraining her impatience,
not to be shaken off even by her. There was no hurrying
Vernon Lee while her inexhaustible mind was at work,
absorbing and straining and philosophising an impression
of beauty, were it the twentieth time that she stood in
that garden and searched its appeal; no experience, be it
ever so familiar, was to be dismissed as finished and
settled in the past, its history was always in the making.
So there was Edith, bright and alert, brisk on her feet
after a winged glance; and beside her Vernon Lee, tall
and angular vestal in her stiff collar and her drab coat,
fixed in rumination, absorbed and unheeding, her rugged
face working in the coil and labour of her burrowing
thought. She pondered, she reconnoitred as she talked;
she wound her way through suggestion, sensation, speculation—she threaded a labyrinth, a branching forest of

shadowy forms; and then again she slashed right and left, she broke into the open with a swinging cut—she thumped out with a judgment, a maxim, a paradox, on a croak or chuckle of her crusted laughter. It all took time, but it was worth while to wait for her. While she talked on, with her pungent and guttural deliberation, a scene unrolled, brilliantly peopled and displayed—a drama was evolved out of all the admonitions, curious and lovely, grand and grotesque, of the genius of this place and this hour. Who will say, listening to Vernon Lee, that a thing of beauty is ever finished or an hour of time accomplished? She knew better; she talked on, planting her weight, as of an elemental earth-force, on any levity or futility of her companions, releasing them with a stroke of her grimly riotous wit—still she talked. Most surprising, most interesting, most exasperating of women, in her power and her humour, her tenacity and her perversity—Vernon Lee holds her ground, to the eyes of memory, in the twinkling ilex-shade of that old garden, as she held it in gnarled and seasoned determination to the end, when her hour was achieved at length. What a figure! Edith admired her, but scarce knew how to treat her. It was impossible to control or to civilise Vernon Lee.

That was a remarkable episode, especially to one who could never have enough of lingering and mooning among Italian shades. But clearly it was not at this measured pace, nor in that time-forgetting mood, that Edith could pursue her journey—least of all in Italy, where she had known her way for so long. The chase was a little breathless, but the excitement grew; there were other worlds, still in Italy, that she threw open to those who clung to her. If we should leave Vernon Lee to her queer crotchets and obstinate questionings, to enter the calm clarity of another circle, overlooking Florence once more—what then? Here was no labouring, no wrestling in the toils of dispute; talk arose, soft-footed and cool, in masterly command of its purpose, with wit that cut without noise, argument tempered and proof, authority absolute and composed. It was the Interpreter's house, with its 'excellent things' for the pilgrim, at which we now arrived—it was Berenson's house, in its fold of the Florentine hills, packed with treasure, crowded with culture. This was that Italy of the new dispensation, Italy beyond the dreams (which in this company it were well to suppress) of the fond sentimentalist: Italy shorn of illusion and mystification, her genius stripped and exposed, and thereby the more honoured. To the rule that is sovereign here, so lucid in its courteous finality, what idle-rambling fancy will fail to bow, for discipline and initiation? It was a spring-time of swift experience for a newcomer. As for Edith, an initiate of years, she breathed freely, she drank of that air with avidity—on that peak of enlightenment, where no visionary vapours stain the sky. I am not sure that she can stay there for long; for where a scholar's work is on hand, ceaseless and soundless, the demands of her restlessness, to deal plainly, are impossible; she soon disarrays a life of order and construction. It matters little, for where will she ever stay for long?—the scholar is well assured that the gale passes. But meanwhile it is pleasant to see her, if only for a glimpse, in a scene where to the end she was so often to be found—in B. B.'s great library, surrounded by the jewels of his store, enthroned among his attendant guests. And so away again to new ground, with the cargo of books freshly stocked, and a companion who could never have enough of ranging and exploring in strange lands.

This time it was ground entirely new to her. When she cast herself upon North Africa, that spring, she was a young discoverer once more, in the bloom of adventure; and when we turned the corner of the road that wound through a mountain-pass, and saw, beyond and beneath, shimmering in silver and grey, the Desert, it was as though mystery and beauty began again from the beginning. It quieted her. I don't think she was very happy in her life at that moment—it may have been a time of particular difficulties. I don't know: certainly nobody would guess there was trouble on her mind, looking only at her rapture of delight in this new world; and yet it was Edith with a difference. If she was tired, here for once she could rest. When she sat in the dusk (as I see her) at our inn-door, in the winding of the pass, watching the white-robed figures that now and then came swinging silent and stately down the road, she sat still and intent—as if she could have sat for ever, alone in the night, breathing some relief, some pacification that she hadn't found in the world she knew so well. And presently she made a discovery that quaintly struck her—it was fresher to her than to most. Small incongruous lump of visibility that we were, descending into the desert with our books and our maps and our imperturbable Cook at the wheel, we seemed to be dissolved— to float as a thin light blur over space and time: a very odd sensation, no doubt, if you have never worn the cap of darkness in your life before. That is what it is to be for once completely isolated in an unknown world that doesn't know you, a world too old to be moved, too vast to be touched, beneath your hand yet out of reach. How

strange again, I remember her saying, the sudden repose, for eyes invisibly watching, of a world where humanity is beauty and nothing else—beauty at every
turn, like that poised figure by the way, slender against
the falling light, Joseph guarding his flock—beauty so
ancient and so young. There was nothing to be taken
from it, nothing to be added to it, and no choice but to
rest for the while in time that stood still. Another night-
piece I recall, the culmination of that unreckoned pause.
At Timgad, under a full moon, in the courts and streets
of the ruined city, dead in the wilderness, there was more
than a spell to pacify a restless mind; and I never forget
how she stood there, lost in the moonlight, silent and
exalted, drawing new life from the unearthly enchantment of that thousand-year-old ghost of the night.

From all this it was a drop and a bump to land once
more in Europe, and in the jostle and indignity of the
quay-side, all too easily knowable and touchable, time
began again. Eye and ear woke up from the peace of
the desert. 'Everyone here,' said one of us, surveying
Europe, 'seems to be doing noisy and ugly and obvious
things; everyone there was doing silent and beautiful
and mysterious things; I want to go back.' There was no
going back; but for a long while, as we went forward,
the vision stayed with us—of the great fawn-coloured
expanses, with the small black unaccountable patch in
the distance that grows and grows and becomes a palm-
oasis—and then the hoarse rattle of the date-palms in
the breeze, the mulberry-coloured children of the dust,
the lean-headed men, the black-swathed women, the
dry faint fragrance, the splash of sun and shade in the
mud-walled lanes: we were sure to go back. And a few
weeks later the storm crashed that scattered the plans

of peace; these were the last days of our old ignorance of a world of war. It was again another Edith who was presently to be seen, active and ardent to new ends; she had taken her draught of rest before the storm, just in time. There was to be plenty more travelling for her later on, and the delight of the road never failed her. But I doubt if often on her journeys she lost touch with her life and her part in the world as she did for a few weeks or hours or moments of that spring—only moments perhaps, but for one so ready in her part they were rare events. Another little aspect of that adventure I mustn't forget; I think that all her many and various fellow-travellers would agree that it was auspicious. In the course of our ranging it befell us not seldom to be lodged for the night in places that might well have provoked that break in the weather of which I spoke just now. But not all: she took the chances of the road, some of them decidedly uninviting, without a word. Once in Europe again she soon returned to herself in this matter; and her companion, remembering Dickens and the Dorrits, might often be inclined to echo the fervent words of Edmund Sparkler, in the inn-yard at Martigny, regarding the remarkably fine woman with no nonsense about her—well-educated too: 'Consequently—why Row?' There was many a row. But she could laugh at herself when it was over, if the laugh was against her; and a certain Spanish scene, described by Mrs. Winthrop Chanler, rose to a level of farce of which the memory was ever enjoyed. Here it is, to close this chapter of her travels.

Twice we travelled together [writes Mrs. Chanler] for a month in Spain. We went in her motor, and she, having seen it all before, arranged two perfect trips, taking in all that could possibly be visited in the given time. Our travels were sometimes clouded by the question of food and lodging. We knew that we must be prepared to rough it if we wanted to cover the Pilgrims' Route; some of the things we most wanted to see were in out-of-the-way places, unprepared for tourist travel. Nevertheless Edith's imagination would run riot over a good word she might have heard about some unexpectedly pleasant little hotel in a certain small town, and the vast difference between what we found and what her mind's eye had pictured led to harsh words with the manager and general distress. Every arrival was made difficult by the fact that the available best was not good enough. On one occasion we reached a straggling hill-town towards evening; I cannot remember its name. Edith had heard of a delightful hotel kept there by two English ladies, gentlewomen who knew what it is to be comfortable; they had taken an old palace and fixed it up with every modern convenience. There was a fine baroque cathedral and bishop's palace; we would visit them next day—it was getting dark, we must find our nice hotel. The only one in sight, the usual Hotel del Comercio, looked very squalid and uninviting. Edith was determined to discover the palace where she was going to find comfort and cleanliness. She knew or thought she knew the name of it. We asked the few people who were about, but no one seemed to have heard of it; all pointed to the Comercio as the only hotel in the place. Finally one rather ruffiantly-looking man whom we accosted showed signs of intelligence. He knew the place, in fact he owned it, and he showed us the way to it, but did not further recommend it as he led us to the door. There was no sign of its being an inn. A blowzy bedizened middle-aged female led us in with a smirking show of cordiality. The house was built round a court, with overhanging balconies or loggias on every floor. The court itself was used as a living-room, messy and unattractive, but evidently a place of amusement. The surrounding loggias opened into more or less private rooms, which sounded occupied. There was an indescribable sense of bad smell about the place. We looked at one another with a wild surmise; it was evidently not for us nor we at all for it. Half amused and entirely disillusioned we made a hasty exit, and put up for the night at the only less loathsome Hotel del Comercio.

IX

Wartime

She had taken a house in England for the late summer of 1914—Stocks, near Tring, the beautiful domain of her friend Mrs. Humphry Ward. I had left her in Paris, after our return from the desert, and if ever I knew her dispirited and dejected it was then, as her own life closed on her once more. From there she had started on another flight—to be soon recalled as she describes in *A Backward Glance*, by the gathering war-cloud. She was in Paris when it broke; but her household had already moved to Stocks, and she presently followed; and there I saw her—a new woman. There was no discouragement in her now, and no repose nor any need of it. Her enthusiasm was like a searchlight, sweeping the scene with a purposeful energy that clearly wouldn't long be contained in those fields of inaction. She was soon in London, and soon joining her ardour to the trumpet-notes of Henry James, who hastened to meet her. They met, as it chanced, over the news of the bombardment of Rheims cathedral, and the outbreak of his wrath had force and resonance to content even her. 'They have begun'—I can still hear his rich proclamation—'but we shall go on—go on till I am seated, with the King of England, the President of France and the Emperor of

Russia—seated upon the stomach of William of Hohen-
zollern, squeezing out the last drop of reparation!' A
weighty settlement! That was the tone for her, the spirit
befitting a clear cause and a straight fight. She was
impatient, I don't say merely of doubtful or devious
hesitation before the challenge of events, but even, as it
seemed, of the need to understand, to search the vast
issue and its implications, and to assemble mind and
thought to face it. She knew no such necessity. One
question alone detained her—what was to be done, and
done by herself; and it was soon answered. Back in Paris
once more she instantly set to work—to work practical
and speedily fruitful; and for the four years to come she
never flagged in it.

Of the detail of her work, what she planned and
accomplished, there is here no need to speak, for the tale
has been told elsewhere; enough to say that it was very
good work, and the best of it designed to outlast that war,
and it is to be hoped another. Not what she did but how
she did it is my concern, and not the direction that her
efforts took, but the promptness, the resourcefulness, the
decision and conviction with which she launched them.
She was and knew herself to be without experience in
organising the work of others; she could stimulate, she
could fire by her example, she could see that nothing
went flat or stale in the doing; and then she could
refrain, having as little love as she had aptitude for the
routine of working days, nor the least desire to take it out
of hands more skilled for it. She found many good helpers
and gave them their opportunity; and especially she soon
found her friends Royall Tyler and his wife, and when
once Mrs. Tyler was in control of the field, the various
fields, of their activity, she herself was free to proceed in

her own way and her own strength—never that of the
director of operations, but always that other, equally
essential, of the brisk influence before and behind, con-
firming and enlivening the course. Her quick generosity
of praise, her no less happy tartness of reprimand, the
rouse and stir of her presence, made it interesting and
eventful to be allied with her, never dull; and anyone
who was ever employed beside or over or under the
volunteers of charitable and merciful works has known
the vital part that is played by such tonic breezes, all the
better if they have their sharpness at times—known too,
what is more, that the best of them are apt to be blown by
a sex unhampered by the prudent responsibility, the re-
gardful discipline, of the peace-loving male. She carried
her part with a will. Her wide circle of connexions,
French and American, supported and enlarged her
action, and she used these too to the full.

I saw her again, stirring and bright-eyed, in the
iron-dark of that first war-winter. Life in the Rue de
Varenne had changed its old ways—but not very much,
after all. The morning walk took her to the office or the
ouvroir, into which she disappeared as promptly as into
the dressmaker's parlour; she swept off on further errands, she scoured the shops for needful supplies, she
interviewed, she inspected; but there was the same
familiar gathering round the evening fire, if there were
gaps in it now, and though the talk had other tones.
Charlie Du Bos was there as usual, but a new Charlie too,
strained with new purpose—all intent, for his part, on the
practical task which he shared with the rest, but intent
with thought and nerve, with feeling and imagination at
stretch; it was not he who could throw himself into war
and its work with but one idea, to get it done. There was

much more in it than that, for him. Now more than ever, among the innumerable ways of doing and feeling and thinking, there was need for the right and best way of all; and if there was so much to explore, and yet something must be done, felt, thought at once, there was bound to be strain. It might be easy for Edith to cut knots; it was a graver matter for so scrupulous and sensitive a brooder. He worked gladly with her, but unlike her he had to receive the whole weight of the catastrophe and dispose of it in his mind and account to himself for its disposal; no wonder he looked tired and sad. Besides— France was wounded, he was France, she but the outraged and devoted friend of France: there is always the difference. She gave in profusion all she had, but it was hers to give; he had nothing to give, for it was he, and he was given and taken by necessity. It is a distinction that is not to be mistaken—in wartime. Anyhow it left her at liberty to lavish her gifts where they were needed; and she ranged ever further among the needs to be met, as far as she could reach them.

It was not very long before she reached the battle-line itself—as she certainly would, we may hold who knew her in peace and war; and it was a great day for her when she was invited, or permitted, to visit a group of military hospitals near the French front, on behalf of the French Red Cross. The hospitals benefited, no doubt; but the greatness of the day was for her in the new field that it opened and the new work that it brought her, entirely in accord with her mind and skill. She saw her chance at once, and made others see; she could here be used in the service of the cause for what she really was, a writer after all. With the best of effect, from this advanced position, she could face her large audience across the ocean, where they waited and looked on; she could speak to them as an eye-witness of France in the fight. For so militant a neutral, and one to whom thousands were ready to listen, what fitter employment could be found? To this end she was allowed, and was among the first to be so allowed, a memorable vision of life at the front, the long entrenched and immobilised front of those years, through repeated visits to posts along the whole of the French line; and it was here, in the freedom and jollity, the confident cheer, the amused give-and-take which received and welcomed her, that she enjoyed her chance. If her hosts were surprised to see her they were pleased to entertain her; for among these men, younger and older, her bearing was perfect, frank and easy and adventurous, and she was passed in good humour and good fellowship from hand to hand. It was open air to breathe—fresh from it she began to write again in earnest; and however she found the time, for she dropped nothing else, long before peace was in sight she had rounded off two highly finished stories, 'Summer' and 'The Marne,' the first looking far away from the war, as well as the series of chapters in which she sketched her impressions of embattled France, caught as they came. So those long middle war-years, while they plodded slowly to the horizon, were lightened for her by striking experience and absorbing pursuits. Her voice carried widely and earned her privileges of increasing interest, that even landed her for a culmination in Africa once more—in Morocco, for a wonderful sight of the future that was building there on a past still strange and secret. And by that time it was not as a neutral, however qualified, that she was serving the genius of France. America had crossed the ocean.

When I saw her once more, still in Paris, in the last of those four war-winters, how much there was to hear and to tell—so far we had all travelled by then, so much we had all learnt and unlearnt since our innocent, ignorant young past of the first war-days. She, with all her adventures upon her, had great tales to tell; but what could be greater than the present, with this new change in the air, the surge of new ardour from the west? To see American uniforms in Paris was a sight for the world; and now it was we others who saw and applauded, their countrywoman who was among them in her right. She was deep in the excitement of the change, that at last was shaking the age-long habit, as it seemed to us all by then, of the fixity and eternity of wartime. When this wind blew, could spring be far behind? Not that she herself, in all that age, had ever been worn down by the grind of it; tired she might be, but not by the pressure of a weight that never lifts; to be tired by variety of vigour, by flights and drops, by zeal and indignation and impatience, this is a very different matter, a fatigue that can leap up to fresh calls, who knows how long?—for as long as they are heard. The other sort of weariness, bowed under its burden, wears another look; it was still Charlie who wore it. He, more strained than ever, had been patiently mining his way through the war, inch by inch, stroke by stroke; he looked up at her with his anxious smile, as she came and went—looked up and shook his head. It isn't over yet, this war; the new uniforms, the rest of us too, have more to learn before we shall have learnt all; we don't yet see the day when the load on our backs will be rolled off whence it came. On deep-seated faith indeed we can live—not on day-to-day hopes, which may fail us to-morrow or any day. But there it is: each of us has his own way of living from one morning of wartime to the next, that everlasting problem we all have to tackle. Nobody can rise above it, but you can be under it or in it, and her way was to be in the thick of it. And somebody in the thick of it who is gay and sensible and helpful at every turn, that one is a treasure indeed as the years drag on, and the best of comrades to the young uniforms. It is pleasant to see them around her—she knew how to talk to them. And if it was possible to wonder what, with all she had seen and heard, she knew of the times we had lived through, under the blows that had battered the world, she could easily retort the question. Did we any of us know so much? *She* knew what the staff-officer told her at the front, what the minister let fall at dinner—and how we all turn to her to hear what it was! There is much to be said for hand-to-mouth, hour-by-hour ways of living for most of us—in wartime.

One note of the times, moreover, it was observable that she had learnt, one that hitherto might seem to have escaped her notice. She had discovered that England was taking part in the war. This was a fact, as I make out, that the slow middle years of the war had obscured—I don't say unnaturally, if there happened to be no one at hand to call attention to it; for the war that she saw, and quite enough too to absorb the mind, was France's war, and whatever was beside or beyond it, especially whatever was beyond the mainland, on the seas of the world, was below the horizon that ringed the war as she saw it. By whom had she been led to look further? I don't know, but I have my idea. There was now a newcomer in the circle of her daily friends, an Englishman; and my suspicion is that this English infusion into the round of her talk and thought had had its effect, steadily and gently pervasive. Anyhow there could be no happier chance than that which brought this friend to Paris and fixed him there for a long sojourn in those times—an emissary of England who doubtless was doing much good there, but nothing better, as it struck me on the spot, than the good he was doing in the Rue de Varenne, where he was familiarly to be seen out of working hours. Well, I must say it was agreeable to hear an English voice there just then—no high-pitched voice, but the quiet firmness in it was unmistakable, as much so as the light of observation and irony in that particular English eye. They were the eye and voice of Eric Maclagan; * and Edith and he, freely enjoying each other's company when work was done, had a way with each other that was pleasing to watch. He knew what he was talking about, and no one knew that, but she listened. The English position, whatever its fortunes elsewhere, could have fallen into no better hands just there and then; and I leave it there without a word, or with no word louder than Eric's which was always attuned to a quick ear. I don't know, as I say; but I hold to my idea that the view of England as seen by Edith, with more lights and shades in it than of old, owed not a little to some of the talk that was to be heard in the Rue de Varenne that winter. There was no great amount of it, however, to be heard by me; and a few weeks later, with the coming of spring, there was revealed, sure enough, what was still to be learnt by us all.

Of the spring when it came, of the summer that followed, of the autumn that fulfilled the year, perhaps

* Now Sir Eric Maclagan, sometime Director of the Victoria & Albert Museum.

none of us, looking back, could easily retrace the marks that are left in a lengthening memory. The war of the mainland, the war that was almost within earshot, the immovable war that had shaped our lives for so long, suddenly heaved and lurched, the huge line swayed and sagged against us—not away from us, but nearer and nearer. Was it possible? Those days of uncertainty—repeated since then with so vast a difference—seem few enough now; they were soon over, but soon to none of us at the time. The swinging weight had been held before long—but had it been held? We were out of the old known war, we were in a new war now, the old landmarks gone. Where *were* we, that summer?—in a new life that there was no time to shape, with new work on our hands, new whirls of thought in our brains—new hopes at last as the summer broadened. But was it possible to see that they were new, when we saw them at last, after those so many old hopes that had failed? How could we be sure of them? So the summer wore on, and the rumour of victory was in the air—not here yet, but approaching; and then indeed the new sound was beyond mistake, unlike any other we had heard before. It came nearer; and one morning the war was over—over so strangely, less with a shout than with an astonished gasp. Was it possible? Peace came like the drop of a noise, a sudden silence in which there was time to think again if you could, but of what could you think?—of what *can* you think, unless it may be of the streaks of silence, reaching back through the noise, that are left in the lives of all?—channels of silence that lead any of us back to moments of wartime that were quiet enough in the enfolding din; in every life over which war passed such moments remain. Here is one, a moment of evening in wartime on which a light now happens to fall:

> Somewhere, O sun, some corner there must be
> Thou visitest, where down the strand
> Quietly still the waves go out to sea
> From the green fringes of a pastoral land.
>
> Deep in the orchard-bloom the roof-trees stand,
> The brown sheep graze along the bay,
> And through the apple-boughs above the sand
> The bees' hum sounds no fainter than the spray.
>
> There through uncounted hours declines the day
> To the low arch of twilight's close;
> And, just as night about the moon grows grey,
> One sail leans westward to the fading rose.
>
> Giver of dreams, O thou with scatheless wing
> For ever moving through the fiery hail,
> To flame-sear'd lids the cooling vision bring,
> And let some soul go seaward with that sail.*

* These verses, dated June 6, 1915, were sent by Edith Wharton to Mrs. George Cabot Lodge, from whom I have received them.

X

Pavillon Colombe

Edith, if no one else, delayed not a moment in beginning again; she at least wasn't found at a loss, surprised by peace. Others in their places, high and low, might stare at the ruins to be rebuilt: there was one bit of construction, in all the tangle and wrangle of those next fevered months, that went forward without a hitch—on the little domain of the Pavillon Colombe, lying round the corner, off the village street of St. Brice-sous-Forêt, some few miles to the north of Paris. This was the retreat to which her life was now to be moved, and she was an example, as usual, to any carver of new states. When she stood among the planks and buckets, the ladders and rubbish-heaps, the universal litter and disorder of restoration, her eye lit up; she saw it all, the invisible shape of the future to be realised, all imaged 'ere mortar dab brick,' and nobody need try to confuse her. See her talking to her architect as she treads the planks in the gutted rooms, and think for a moment how we most of us appear in that plight: how we follow him gaping, feebly agreeing with his explanations, stifling the faint misgiving at the back of the mind—is it really turning out as I meant?—but oh, yes, yes, I quite see that it must be as you say (I wonder why!). I have the deepest sympathy with the world-repairers at their congress. Here we behold a master tackling the job, and for my part I watched her open-mouthed. How could she be so sure that her life wouldn't match the invisible whole if this weren't changed, that abolished—this partition redrawn, that corridor extended? There was no shadow of doubt about any of it—those who receive her decree may make up their minds to that. I remembered what Henry James had once said: 'No one fully knows our Edith who hasn't seen her in the act of creating a habitation for herself.' Certainly it was a very charming place that she had found for her art to work on—even in its chaos that was clear: a distinguished little mansion of the eighteenth century, exquisite and discreet, with romantic and scandalous associations—scandal and romance together of perfect elegance, united in high style; not a style to which we could all of us subdue our romances or correct our scandals, but with the softness of age upon it, relaxing its deportment, the grace of its welcome is enlarged, and there is room in it for our more easy-going age. The successor of the Demoiselles Colombe, who dwelt here of old in all the taste of their day, smiled back at them with amused friendliness, and refashioned their abode to suit herself.

A few months later it was done, and by the summer's end the Pavillon Colombe was safe in the hands of her good ministers, Gross and White. The guest, dropping into his place prepared, found the new life running as noiselessly as though it had known no check or change. The house was perfect in every corner, and not the house only, but the garden too; for even a garden, it was now to be seen, showed no unruliness under her hand. Before the low white house—which, as you en-

tered the big doors of the side-court, turned its back
once for all on the outer world—there now lay the neat-
est of parterres, soberly patterned in green, with no
flowers to scatter the sunshine that brimmed its enclosure; and then a grove of great trees, with a shadowy
basin of water in the midst; and beyond again the open
breadth of the *potager,* where abundant flower-borders
framed the trim kitchen-stuff and drilled lines of fruit-
espaliers spread their arms; and the whole domain, compact within its girdle, was all privacy and seclusion,
ordered to the right scale for dignity within its bounds.
And the same indoors: there were big rooms that were
small enough, small rooms that were big enough, a long
row of them on both the two floors, facing the sun-
brimmed parterre, with all the garden-airs and garden-
noises, fresh and light, pervading them—a sanctuary
dressed, if ever there was one, like that of Keats, 'with
the wreath'd trellis of a working brain.' And the day's
life too, within its setting, was as complete in its round:
reaching out to the leafy walks of the neighbouring
forests, Montmorency and Ecouen—with no errands
here to detain you, no doorways to be left in—and the
constant car-excursions, that radiated ever farther in
the freedom of the country; closing in for the familiar
sessions in the long brown library, a graver and more
thoughtful room, no less point-device, than the saloon
of the Rue de Varenne; and now, for a new element in
the day, the care of the garden, ever in need of snipping
and trimming, and its enjoyment when trimmed and
snipped—though its idle enjoyment the guest on the
whole might ensue by himself, for Edith seemed always
to like admonishing and edifying her garden rather than

conversing with it, well as they evidently understood each other too. And sufficient as they appeared from the first, these early impressions were to grow and spread with every visit as the years went on, and the precinct widened its embrace for new recesses and alleys and orchard-expanses—always crowned and dominated by the great elms in the midst, arching the pool, where high overhead, all through the summer morning, an oriole fluted with its lovely bell-voice, the voice of a 'branchèd thought,' last enchantment of the sanctuary. Such was the Pavillon Colombe, as Edith shaped and dressed it.

And for herself as she lived in it, with her friends and her books and her daily work, the new order of things might well seem as good as the old, and better; for here she was now on country soil of her own (it could just be said, if only just, that St. Brice was out of town), and her joy in the country, though you felt she always had her eye on its behaviour, was deep and true. And when she now stood on the good soil of her garden, with her broad-leafed hat and her basket on her arm, calling and waving to the window where Gross looked out and smiled proudly down on her; or when she whisked round and made off to her business among the flowers, with her pair of toy dogs sputtering and scuffling at her heels ('those damned Pekinese,' says G. L. roundly); or when, her basket filled, she stepped out, young as ever in the straightness and lightness of her attack, for a further survey of the garden's diligence—with that neat right-and-left twitch of her elbows as she stepped, and that 'elegant manner of moving and placing her feet' (says another observant friend) 'that always reminded me of the exquisite nicety with which a small donkey picks its way and places its feet on a stony path' * (there's a quick glimpse!): in short, wherever you first caught sight of her, active and occupied, in this new picture of her creation, this design of order and beauty she had conjured from her brain, she seemed to be settling down to peace in the world with the happiest assurance that everything round her, all for which *she* need answer, was right and fair, a field sufficient and convenient for good work through the years to be. Where indeed would you find a life more fitly renewed, with its broad fringe of amenity carried so lightly, while so carefully, not weighted or hampered by it?—with room for concentration, time for diversion—with bevies of friends within hail, not too near, to come dropping in at their appointed hour for the amusement of the garden's repose. They dropped in, they admired, throwing up their hands with their pretty phrases of appreciation over the delight of the place and the charm she has wrought in it—tribute graciously acknowledged, if its ring isn't altogether in tune with the mind of the garden, that is no Trianon play of rustic make-believe; but it is soon forgotten when silence falls on the trees in the dusk, and all the windows and doors of the house stand open, as the lamps light up within, to the largeness of the country night. Here, to be sure, is a writer of books propitiously installed; and how satisfying to think of a writer in the midst of it all, enjoying it all—and then forgetting it all, alone with her book, at the true centre of the whole design.

Was Edith Wharton that writer? We have long known her a serious and practical craftsman, as she

* I thank Mrs. R. P. Nicholson for the charming exactitude of this comparison.

faced her book in those guarded hours of the morning;
and now, when you think of her at work in her pavilion
of art, you might see in her the happy writer that we
all, driving our pens, should wish to be. To honour
your craft and to know your hand—what more do you
need?—and if more, then certainly she had more in
plenty. I never heard of her deranged in her work by
troublesome moods, or left high and dry, between page
and page, by any distemperature of the brain; the lis-
somness of her mind, the head and push of her fancy, she
seemed able to count upon these without question. And
not only the book was always firm under her hand, but
other books, more and more, were continually calling
to her and asking to be written; they were importunate
with their cries and claims. She complained that she
couldn't open her window, pausing at a full stop, but
other subjects, appealing *données*, came fluttering in
to distract her; never was a writer so beset by books un-
born, to be gently pushed aside to leave room for the
book in the making. Here indeed is a fortunate writer
at work, enjoying herself; the rest of the world can
wait, she needs it not. She does not—for an hour or two,
while the door is shut: but what then? Is the world ever
kept waiting, shall we ask once more, when she emerges,
her book put by till to-morrow? I am not suggesting
that the earnestness of a writer is to be esteemed by the
rapt gaze, the flashing eyes and floating hair, round
which the world knowing its place, weaves circles
thrice. But a writer is a writer, surely we may hold,
when he not only knows a good friend in his work,
but will rely on that friend, if need be, for company,
for reassurance, for all the validity and consistency of
his being; 'I *could* manage,' he says, 'with nothing but

that to save me.' Edith Wharton, no doubt, never to that length confided herself to the friend in her work; she always had, she felt she had, to take other precautions, to provide herself with everything else within reach—and there was so much within her reach. Well, I only mean, after all, that when she sat at her work she faced a companion whom she loved and trusted, but one who never was, never had the chance to be, all the comfort and cheer that she required. Her companion, I could fancy, had no illusions on this head—but may have thought he could have done more for her all the same, first and last, than she was willing to believe.

But then she was a novelist, and a painter of humanity can't live on himself and his lonely virtue; the imagination of a novelist is a maw that must perpetually be crammed. Haven't we seen, for that matter, in the master of the art whose genial comment we have so often caught in passing—seen in Henry James himself a denizen of the world so attentive, so massively and ceremonially studious of its style and form, that he even incurs the charge (which doesn't trouble him at all) of taking it more seriously than it deserves—that urbane world of his choice, which he makes his province? Even Edith declared (so G. L. tells me, but he may be granting her his own wit) that the souls in Henry's breast were three, souls of a genius, of an angel, and of Major Pendennis: a clever saying, whichever said it, but it gives the novelist no trouble, for it is not the Major's world that matters, it is what happens to it in Henry James—and he alone knows the eventful history that dignifies it in his brain. It is the cause, the high cause of the maker, turning fact into truth, chance into fate, windfalls of no worth into apples of gold, which has all the importance that is anywhere to be confessed. As for Edith herself, with the world awaiting her, she at least would never be charged with any solemnity in her regard, any compliance in her affability: do but watch her as she advances to take her place! She spares herself no pains, as we know, while she occupies her place; but the patient observer, the watchful absorber of the scene is elsewhere, pressed by the throng— not where *she* is, cynosure of the assembly, free to extend a gracious and inviting hand; and in a minute or two, in an hour or so, she has turned her back and is gone. Her glance is quicker than any where it falls, more inquisitive and more divining; but no student she, no brooding analyst persevering in a research. Nor was she ever, what is more, a sociable spirit enjoying the mere commerce of her kind, thriving on the currency of general intercourse; on the contrary, as we have learnt, the crowd scared her as a crowd—she couldn't be quite herself or perfectly keep her head in it, if you knew how to interpret the signs of her discomposure. Alike for interest and for delight, the populous scene could never satisfy her need—there was always a pull in her mind that held her back from its familiarity; she would rather hear tell of the world, when it came to the point, than loosely mix with it. And yet she must have it, she wasn't complete without it; and still in her attitude towards it, in her dealing with it, there was this quarrelling strain, this tease of she will and she won't, of dependence and defiance. There were times, in the garden of the pavilion, when it was plain to see.

It was seen most tellingly, but in a special light, changing its appearance, when she talked with men— with more, that is, than one man at a time, for with one at a time the case was simpler. With a man, then, on each side of her, let alone with others in the offing, I can believe that a novelist might have returned that clever stroke upon herself. Two souls at any rate there were in her then; I won't try my wit for an epigram, but I might describe them. The first was the soul of a friend, equal in fellowship, frank and free—of a bold and generous sharer of life, wherever it found its like—life that clears the air, works its mind, trusts its senses and isn't afraid of its shadow. I can't imagine a straighter or sounder pact than this that was sealed on the spot, without any ado, in the clasp of a hand—if it could be left at that. But the other soul couldn't leave it—the other soul was irrepressible; and back we come, away from the open and its chances, the same for us all, to the picture of a lady in her garden, circled by her due of masculine attendance, holding her court. It was a scene of high comedy, of the highest indeed, where all the points of a classic tradition were made and taken—at least when played by a company that had the tradition in its blood. There are races, it is known, less polished in their taste, tribesmen of an insular savagery who aren't so fluent in their parts; and to speak for one of them, looking on from the wings, it was of schoolday memories that he was often irresistibly reminded. It might be long since I, a biddable fag, last heard the call which sends us flying on the errands of the great; but I heard it again, quite unmistakable, when Edith commanded the service of her court. She would look round, conscious of her title, her prerogative; and then, over her shoulder, 'Lower boy!' she cried—or so it sounded to me; and if the call wasn't answered with alacrity—if there were any so ungallant as to shirk it, which did happen at

times (yes, I catch several eyes)—she couldn't understand it at all, and showed as much. The tradition was
in *her* blood, sure enough, and it held her fast. To take
things as they came, the rough with the smooth, a friend
among friends, and chance the offhand mixture—she
could do so, and yet again she couldn't; and across her
tolerance, her comradely freedom, there fell this clash
once more, the same old quarrel—trifling indeed, yet
not always so trifling, and anyhow never finally composed. There was something in all this to be considered—
first, no doubt, with a smile and a look of understanding
that passes from eye to eye among her friends, who don't
mind recalling how she liked to marshal her fags: but
then with a different thought, one that goes deeper into
the life of a woman who, with all that she possessed,
possessed only the world that others share. It is easy
perhaps to hold them lightly, your rights and dues in
the world, when you have something of your very own,
were it only a memory, proof in its kind, to ensure your
ground as a human being and to settle you in peace, safe
with yourself. Otherwise there is a gap to be defended,
a point of insecurity to be made good, and the means of
reassurance must be sought and taken as you find them.
The glance of understanding between her friends may
change its expression as they look back and remember
a lonely woman.

All the more, year by year, she counted on the company of a few who remained when the rest dispersed.
They remained, and not so few, with others joining them
as time went on—friends of an inner ring. But she had
reached the age, nearing sixty as she was, when older
friendships, those that contain the past, begin to vanish,
carrying with them the past that is not bequeathable to

their successors. Two of the older and of the very best are henceforth to be seen no more: Henry James was gone, Howard Sturgis soon followed. Of these two and of all they were to her there is worthy commemoration in the pages of her *Backward Glance;* and now, in later retrospect, she herself can never be far from either. The first of them for many years had been the greatest among her friends—the greatest, not the oldest, nor the closest, nor the most influential; he was not of those who had coloured or swayed the mind of her youth. She had made friends with him in her books, so to speak, when she began to write—enrolled, as was evident, under his banner, a disciple of his art; but of his authority, as she emerged from pupilage, she was by no means patient, nor a meek receiver of his doctrine—though his approval of her work, when she got it, was the only meed of praise that she greatly cared about or valued. Nor, beneath the benignity of his observant eye, was there any filial deference in her mien; there was no ceremony in her affection. Rather he was, in her life, a wide region of inexhaustible abundance, larger and richer than any other, from which there was ever more and yet more to be harvested. He was nonsuch, and while he lived there was always that big liberal genius to feast upon—a banquet spread, with laughter perpetually with him, over him, at him, all magnified by his own. Such plenty there was of him, moreover, that could never be lost, the store of him that his friends possessed and kept. And as for Howard Sturgis, while he lived, there was the link of perhaps the rarest confidence of all, the friend to whom it was easiest to say what can never be said—easiest to be yourself, however you were, and to be understood as that. A tie so living and so personal,

[146]

with the current that flows in it—this may be the kind
most plainly lost when it is gone. Howard too left much
behind him, but this he couldn't leave, the instant accord of his understanding; and when he was gone and
the current severed, he was gone indeed—only the loss
endured. And so these two are to be heard no more;
neither of them ever saw that garden of the pavilion,
where they were so often recalled and missed when the
few were left to themselves. Upon these who remained
she could always count—she had only to ask for what
they had to give. They couldn't give her more than she
could take; and the power to rest, negligent and un-
strung, she could take from no one, if she began to know
at last that she wanted it.

Did she want, or ever know that she wanted,
younger life of her own about her—the children she
hadn't missed of old? It was an obvious question to ask,
and she was not one to ask an obvious question, even
of herself; I doubt if she knew, or allowed herself to
know, what the answer would have been. If the answer
was given notwithstanding, and clearly enough, it appeared in less simple a guise. She disliked children, it
was generally declared—again perhaps too simply; for
one of her friends, herself a mother, speaks with insight
of 'Edith's rare gift of treating children as normal human beings,' * one by one, not as the small and in-
distinguishable fry which they so consciously are not. If
to like children is to like them all, anyhow and everywhere, it was a more discerning and more gratifying
attention that she paid them when they came her way—
which was not, as it chanced, very often, but there were
a few with whom she had a friendly and humorous al-

* Mrs. Walter Maynard.

liance that is pleasantly remembered. And still more art-
lessly again—how, it was sometimes wondered, had she
learnt to know so well the children in her books, where
they are a lively pack, and where their shrewd and sensitive portrayal is a striking grace? Boys and girls, great
or small, have rarely been drawn with a more transparent
felicity than by this woman who made no cult of them
and had none of her own. Is that surprising? It would be
more so, after all, if a childless writer had never been a
child; and this was one who knew the world of a child,
and could live in it again, by clear lights of memory and
imagination. But that was the safe world of the past;
and in the present, no doubt, the sight of the place filled,
the attention claimed, by the world's young brood was
a much more questionable affair. She regarded it with
curiosity, with resentment, and with something like
dismay. I needn't try to thread the tangle of her feeling
in this matter: another friend cuts a straight way through
it. 'I have seen her,' says Mrs. Chanler,

> really frightened in the presence of children. With
> all her great intelligence she knew nothing of the
> natural pleasure our children give us; she inter-
> preted maternal devotion as heroic self-sacrifice—
> indeed she seemed to look on all family life as more
> or less of a calamity. I often told her that if ever
> the story of her life came to be written in the form
> of the lives of the saints in the Second Nocturn, we
> should learn that the devil frequently appeared to
> Edith Wharton in the shape of a little child, but
> he was never able to deceive her as to his true
> nature—she was always well aware of it, and
> eschewed all contact with him under that disguise.

This is keenly said, and the humour of it may suggest the answer to the question asked just now—the answer that is not so obvious. They made a pretty picture, the children in the house; it touched and moved her—it chafed and ruffled her. The inference, it may be granted, is clear enough, and the question answered; but I doubt she never looked it in the face.

As for her old home, her old ties, the life she had left behind her in America—on all this ground the tangle had by now become a thorn-thicket, in which it would be rash for me to adventure alone; but I follow a broad back.

Her whole attitude towards America [says G. L.], after she had definitely left it, was enigmatical. It preoccupied and interested her in many ways, and for many and sometimes contradictory reasons; yet in intimate talk with me (and I dare say with other American friends) she habitually expressed the strongest aversion to it. She did not realise and was not prepared to believe that there was much left of the America she valued, although it couldn't be had as you might say over the telephone—least of all by a woman in a hurry. Indeed it really exasperated her to find that as soon as my summers were at my own disposal I began to pass them regularly at home. She professed to make nothing of the fact that I had three generations of my immediate family in those parts, not to mention a good many old and close friends, and occasionally spoke with such impatience, not to say asperity, that I took care to avoid the subject; she couldn't ever approach it without a slight rise in temperature. Yet when I came back she always wanted to hear what I could tell her about where I had been and whom I had seen. The fact is that she could neither do with contemporary America nor do without it; she could neither forget nor forgive it; and as I don't think she had ever analysed or even stated the problem, her conscience was uneasy and her tongue sometimes bitter. On the other hand the older American memories that we had in common, the New York scene of the eighties, the food, the theatre, the dress, the 'protocol,' the old societies of Boston and Lenox—these held her with kindly interest, and were matter for laughter that was free from ridicule. After my yearly visit to Newport, where there were still numbers of her cousins and contemporaries, and where I happened to know the occupants of the houses she had lived in as a girl and after her marriage, I usually had to face more questions than I could answer, when I saw her next, though I had foreseen and tried to prepare myself for a pretty close examination.

So G. L. brings light into the thicket, and much that was obscure grows intelligible in the clearance.

I think, for example, of her insatiable appetite for the horrid details of the invasion of her own world— her droll and dear old world that was perishing, as she saw it, under the trampling of strange new legions. She loved, I must say she loved, to cherish her disgust, or to rasp her amusement, with the report, always at a due distance, of the freaks and frolics of these intruders— how they crashed into the haunts of ancient peace, cackling their outrageous idiom, spilling their monstrous millions ('slopped about' with a vengeance): till a friend

was inclined on occasion to put the plaintive question—
why, if we dislike it all so much, shouldn't we change the
subject? She couldn't say why; but the subject seemed
undying, even in her books. And now I see in it, over
G. L.'s shoulder, a counter-irritant against the scratch of
uneasiness that he detects—the twinge of a consciousness
that she was shirking deeper and more vital claims. She
had all too summarily cut her own roots, and wouldn't
admit that you can't do that and continue to draw the
sap of sound experience. And yet for that too she han-
kered—she missed that natural sustenance. After all it
was still there in its place, the home of her past, firm on
its feet if its head was topped by newer growth; and she
might excuse her neglect of it by declaring that it had
ceased to be—in her heart she knew that it wasn't her
home that had ceased, it was her intimacy, her community with it that had languished. At any rate she knew
enough of the stout survival of her own world to desire
its countenance; she had no thought of disclaiming its
good opinion, whether or no she invariably had it. And
not only as a daughter but as a novelist of New York,
where was she now?—in the air, more and more, it must
be confessed, with scanty means of replenishing her
native store. Very little of the stuff of experience is
needed, she always maintained, a grain here, a pinch
there, to raise a beanstalk of the best in the right imagination—as indeed she had signally proved, time and again,
in some of her strongest work. And still the doubt remained: how long may a novelist hope to nourish his
book on an impression, a sensation, a feather-weight
caught in the air, and nothing more? It was an uneasy
question on all sides, this of her American bearings. But
again there is always the past—the kindly and unquar-

relsome past, ever ready to live and stir anew in its soundless play behind the sheet of glass that preserves and protects it. She was safe with the past, and it was safe with her; she wouldn't suffer it to be mocked by anything but the tenderness that understood. The past too had its room in her books, away from the clatter of the 'Hotel Nouveau Luxe'—a better room for good work, when all is said.

On the whole, I conclude, it was scarcely wonderful if her trellised pavilion, for all the art of its creation, showed signs of unseen strains and tensions within. I don't know, nor pretend to say, how it seemed to her in solitude; but if it was solitude that she chiefly dreaded and evaded, the fact tells its tale. Whatever else there was in it, at least the signs upon the surface, for others to see, were neither strange nor serious. I have spoken of some of them, and one more glimpse will suffice. Here we are then, a group of friends upon the lawn, sitting in the shade, having our talk out, with the long summer evening before us, the picture of ease. With Edith in the midst, urging the talk and leading it such a dance, her ready laughter flying ahead of it—with Edith to keep us all in play, so that we surprise ourselves with our own daring, our flashes and flings—it is indeed a pleasant settlement and a lovely evening. We seem to have hours before us, with our minds slipping free, our fancies broadening in the serene of the sundown, while the garden hums and dreams. But can it last? Somehow there is that in the air, clear as it looks, which distracts our surrender to the charm. It might last for ever—if it weren't for those things that begin to happen: if it weren't for those blessed toy dogs, always whining and complaining about something, so that Edith has to pounce and chide and console; or if she hadn't forgotten some needed object that one of us (which is it to be?) must be despatched to find; or if her eye weren't caught by some misdemeanour of the flower-beds, to be instantly corrected; or if she hadn't herself disappeared into the house, for something else forgotten or remembered, throwing the talk upon our hands before we know she is gone. It can't last: in vain the garden invites to sociable repose; it is not a place in which life will stand still, or the moment stay to be possessed. One must always be girt for movement; sometimes we feel that we must skim the ground, like Alice, to remain where we are. It was a good joke, and one to be made the most of—the restlessness of this wild woman in her leisure; it was the theme of a jest with many variations. But here is enough of it, and those who are left to talk of her may talk rather of the gallantry of an attempt to keep a life whole and brave, single-handed, head high and colours flying, that was a life with a want at its heart, perhaps with a wound. Once more it is Charlie Du Bos, standing a little apart, with his air of puzzled gravity, not joining in the joke, who seems to see the farthest. He, as we know, was never afraid of a too familiar quotation. 'The little less, and what worlds away': the words live again in his pensive tone, full of their meaning.

XI

Through eyes of France

You ask me [writes Madame Saint-René Tail-landier] for some recollections of our friend Mrs. Wharton, and your request answers a thought that has been with me ever since her death—the thought that I too, when the time came, might add my own small tribute to the rest in doing honour to her memory. I was never myself an intimate friend of hers. We had few points of contact in our daily lives; we differed in race and faith, in habit and experience; indeed we were contrasted at every point, and our friendship was founded on what we divined of each other much more than on what we said. For my part I like this reserve; it had a kind of greatness on her side, and it implied a mutual understanding. We met, so to put it, in the open, in a garden of the mind, among the choice roses of her growing, the homelier violets of mine; and there we talked at large of other 'garden-fancies,' curious and far-fetched, the works of our literary friends. My image is at any rate one that well beseems her. Which of us all who knew her, however slightly, can recall her name without the vision of a garden, perfect in its beauty?

Madame Saint-René Taillandier, in her graceful response to the request made to her, thus strikes the very note that is appropriate at this point. It is the moment for a view of Edith Wharton in a new light, a sight of her through eyes most friendly, but eyes that saw her with a difference, in another perspective. The friends who visited her in her pavilion were very many, and many among them were those who talked with her, thought of her, regarded her, in French, the French of their blood; and here is one who knew and admired her, but who knew her always a foreigner in France of the French, tending her exotic blossoms with an art to be divined, not wholly to be explained. This friend, at home in her own France, might well wonder how it was to be an alien on that ground, the most deeply worked, most inexhaustibly fructifying of Europe, and the most jealously entailed to the children of the blood: an alien, moreover, to all appearance so assured and acclimatised in her settlement. How Edith seemed to such eyes as these it must be interesting to learn, and has not yet been heard. We know how Charlie Du Bos watched her, himself confessedly a little in doubt as he sought to penetrate her guard; but *his* doubts were all his own, a personal concern, not the hesitations of one who mainly saw her, as was natural, in these racial crosslights. Between Edith and Charlie, between Edith and many other close friendships that she possessed in France, such typical notes of contrast were as nought, long lost in familiarity; but there were many more around her who knew her well, yet not so well as to have forgotten the distance from which she had arrived. And now, as they speak of her, the shade of reserve in their relation, the light brush of surprise, has a revealing effect of its own, like the chance sight of a well-known figure caught in the field of a mirror, touched with strangeness. The garden of the pavilion, then, is now cleared of us all who think in English; and this is Edith freshly and pleasantly reflected—Edith as *we* never saw her, but it is she to the life.

First, however, comes the little comedy, highly characteristic of those concerned, that was to be played out before the scene could be reached.

I was late [continues Madame Saint-René Taillandier] in getting to know her, though it is now twenty years ago. An odd train of circumstances—odd but not rare: I have known the like in other connexions—had kept us apart. We were both of us close friends of Paul Bourget and his wife. Between the Bourgets, my husband and myself, there were old ties of brotherly intimacy and affection; we sometimes spent weeks together at a time, quite informally, in the country or abroad; we saw each other at all hours, we discussed all subjects. Bourget, who was contradiction itself, was very fond of me, but loved to scold me for what he called my nonsensical ideas: 'Madeleine is crazy' implied no censure as he said it. He and my husband were old school-friends, on the easiest terms, and his wife and I were as sisters-in-law, received by marriage into their fraternity. And speaking of gardens, there was one that the Bourgets kept strictly to themselves, a private (though not at all a secret) enclosure of which those without might only catch glimpses through the locked gate; it was the garden of certain friendships which they guarded as personal and exclusive possessions of their own—Maurice Barrès and his wife, for example, were there, and Mrs. Wharton. It was a peculiarity of theirs—not unknown, as I say, in others—and it was a matter of amusement to the rest of us. Sometimes we cheated in fun and peeped over the fence; we knew it was forbidden. The Bourgets had no children, nor any family about them, and they regarded these special friendships with the touch of possessive jealousy that most of us, knowingly or not, devote to our own 'belongings.' There was to be no sharing, then; the more they cherished their friends, the less they allowed them to make friends with one another. At the same time they delighted in extolling the charms and perfections of each one to the rest; never was anyone comparable to this or that friend of theirs— whom we might meet some day, whom we never did meet, and who ended by becoming a figure of romance. I was myself more than once surprised and confused to discover what an idealised portrait had been drawn of me by the man who was never tired of scolding and threatening me with disaster for my follies; and I wondered what could be thought of me when the portrait was compared with the original.

Thus it was that for fifteen years, over the paling of the guarded enclosure, I heard tell of 'our friend Edith Wharton'—of her beauty, her talent, her fame in America, her gardens in France, the hill-terraces of her lovely Sainte-Claire in the south. One detail in particular, I remember, fired me with a desire to see Sainte-Claire for myself. I was told

how the tiled paths were bordered with hyacinths,
alternately blue and pink, all of which had to bud
and blossom in harmony together, at the right moment, to adorn her paradise. I own that I listened
to these descriptions with a certain impatience.
I felt that a poor unknown like myself, weighted
with a whole paraphernalia of husband, children,
governess, furniture, to be carted from one diplomatic post to another, with all the cares of a family
and a career in which the wife has to bear her share
of the burden, could never aspire to the slightest
contact with this great and still invisible angel,
'our friend Edith Wharton.' In short I was thirty
when I began to think of Mrs. Wharton, and I
was nearly forty-five when for the first time we met.
It was at the dress rehearsal of a play of Bourget's,
and we were all five of us there, my husband and I,
the Bourgets, and their American friend. And what
came of it? Nothing whatever. Perhaps it is embarrassing for two people to have known each other
so well for fifteen years without knowing each other
at all. I had dreamed of the great angel among her
pink and blue hyacinths, I had read the novels that
revealed her as a writer; I knew she had followed
me and mine, by means of our friends, through our
various diplomatic fortunes; and now two women
sat together at the play, with nothing to exchange
but a few mild platitudes. 'Are you staying long in
France?' 'Do you like your time in Portugal?' (My
husband was then minister there). 'I should love
to see America.' Ships that pass in the night!

So it continued for a long time: chance meet-
ings, few and far between—congeniality, perhaps

curiosity on both sides. And then one day, after our return to France, I received a letter from Hyères. Mrs. Wharton informed her 'chère Madame' that she was not satisfied with a translation of *The Age of Innocence* intended for the *Revue des Deux Mondes:* did I happen to know of 'a person' who would undertake to revise and correct the work and put it into good French style?

My first thought was entirely against the idea. It seemed to me rash indeed to correct the work of another; between author and translator and reviser the result could be nothing but a patchwork. Better, surely, to begin again from the beginning and risk an entirely new version. I had not reached the end of my reflections when I found that a large parcel had been left for me with my concierge. It was the manuscript of the novel, and I understood at once who was meant by the 'person.' My daughter had just translated Galsworthy's *Man of Property*, a piece of work that had kept us all employed in a happy hunt for words and phrases and equivalent expressions; and I doubt not that the Bourgets had spoken of it to Mrs. Wharton as a masterpiece. My brother, André Chevrillon, Anglicist-in-chief of our family, had helped with advice and searching criticism, in his enthusiasm and affection for the English novelist. Mr. Galsworthy himself came one evening and spent several hours with us over the work, when it was nearly finished; and I can truthfully say that in his sober and charming manner he showed himself pleased and even astonished at his transformation. He knew our language well, but not so well as to be prepared for what is so familiar to us, its verbal and rhythmic wealth. 'I seem never to have understood myself so well,' he said, 'as in your translation.'

And so I said to my daughter, 'we shall never find the "person" Mrs. Wharton asks for; nobody will care to tackle the work in that fashion at second-hand. But we might undertake it ourselves—the more so because I am convinced that that was at the back of her mind. She was too discreet to say so, but she didn't even wait for my answer to send the manuscript. Let us read it, and do it together.' So said, so done. We took the book chapter by chapter, working separately, comparing and rewriting; we read what we had done and put it back on the stocks. Finally Mrs. Wharton invited us both to St. Brice, to join her in putting the finishing touches. Then only, in 1921, I really knew her.

My daughter and I had thoroughly enjoyed our work, and we became friends with the author on the spot. I knew nothing of America and its modern manners, which attracted my curiosity more than my liking; but *The Age of Innocence,* with its air of the past, its touches of old puritanism, the old Dutch settlers' names, had a quality of its own that greatly appealed to us both. There were many delightful hours at St. Brice, hours of free and frank discussion that flew like minutes; the house became a workshop of craftsmen, intent upon their job. Mrs. Wharton knew our language as well as we did, yet not as we did from within, as a natural inheritance from childhood, and she made discoveries that at times surprised and enchanted her. 'Where ever did you hit on that?' she would cry. 'Why, in nursery tales, schoolgirl memories, family dramas of our own; remember we have always lived in French, a very different matter from knowing it even to perfection.' We agreed that English has its own peculiarities of style—simple and familiar in the novel, quite another in poetry, another again, nearer to French, or rather Latin, in dissertation and rhetoric. The English novel in particular, trans- posing the everyday speech of ordinary people, ad- mits a blurred and colloquial freedom that would be quite out of place in French; if you translate too literally you find its ordinary language becoming extraordinary indeed. And so we adopted a pro- cedure that much amused her. We began by trans- lating, book in hand, closely following the text, with odd and often absurd results; then, closing the book and forgetting that there had ever been a text in English, we set about re-writing our own version. * So only, as it seemed to me, through French on French, is real French to be reached at last.

Those were delightful afternoons, evenings too sometimes, in the soft-coloured library, with the low tables covered with new books, the flower-paintings on the walls, the door wide open to the garden and its scents, the bowls of great poppies or blue lark- spurs, shedding their petals, or a tall white lily, alone in a crystal jar, in noiseless attendance. Then, as the hours passed, under a spell of self- forgetfulness, I became aware of Edith's inner spirit, stirring beneath her admirable control—a

* Excellent method followed in the translation of these very pages. (P.L.)

kind of resonance from within, betrayed by a restless movement or an impatient tone. There was no
need to talk of ourselves; in our search for phrases
and shades of meaning we talked of the people in
the book, and revealed ourselves in doing so. They
were all there in the room, explaining their distinctions. 'Don't forget that I am Dutch by descent,'
remarked the grandmother of the clan: 'I don't be-
have like my Americanised grandchildren.' 'Don't
treat *me* as if I were Dutch,' cried the grand-
daughter: 'we have been settled here for seventy
years!' Such was indeed the very theme and argument of the book—the transformation, so to speak,
of flowers planted in a strange soil, crossing and
evolving into a new race.

It was a mark of our hostess, whether natural
or self-imposed, that when the hours of work were
over, there was an end: the book-people vanished,
the luncheon-bell rang, and there was only a hostess receiving her friends with all the arts of civilisation. Not a trace now of the writer, not the faintest
allusion to her books, the praise they had won, the
criticism they had excited; one dropped into the
habit of never speaking, almost of never thinking
of them in her presence. It struck me one day that
this absolute rule of hers, never to allow talk of
herself, had been adopted at the expense of her
natural feelings as an artist. I had read in the correspondence of Melchior de Vogüé, recently published, some words of high praise of *The House of
Mirth*. I showed Edith the passage and noticed her
quick start. 'Ah, if only he had told me that when
he was alive!' she said, with what I felt was a

pang of regret for sympathy unspoken and lost.

Shall I make a confession? The perfection of her taste, extending to everything, even to the smallest details of her establishment, the arrangement of the flower-beds, the symmetry of the hedges, the neat ranks of the trees in the orchard— sometimes, when I was too conscious of it all, it chilled me. I am allowed in these pages to speak freely, and you see I do so. I have often noticed, among Americans attracted by our civilisation and our traditions, something for which we ourselves are scarcely prepared, something that exceeds our measure—almost, in the English phrase, 'too much of a good thing.' In nearly every French interior you will notice a clock that betrays the bad taste of the mother-in-law, or a woolwork chair-cover, touching relic of 'bonne-maman.' With Mrs. Wharton I was intimidated by the esthetic perfection of everything about her; I felt that if I had made any sort of mistake in my appearance that clear eye would observe it, without appearing or even wishing to do so. The society that surrounded her seemed to be composed of artists, writers, travellers, diplomats, people of culture, French, English and American—always a few at a time, without the added weight, never to be evaded by us in our homes, of family ties. Never what *we* call 'a dinner,' nor even that rage of the Parisian world, 'a tea,' where a hundred and fifty people meet in a stream with a passing 'how do you do?' and a hasty word interrupted by the next 'how are you?' With Edith you found a real circle of men and women who liked each other's company; talk flowed between friends who had travelled far and wide, often together, who could discuss their experience of half a dozen countries and compare notes on all the sights and galleries of Europe and the United States. There was no trace, moreover, of the clique reserved for the initiate and their mutual admiration; nothing could be freer and more disinterested than these small gatherings, from which all professional marks and party labels were banished. What might perhaps be missed was a little spontaneous gaiety, and perhaps this too might be due to something in the character of our hostess, at least during the time when I knew her. In her perfect poise there was a certain impassivity. I never heard her say she was sad or depressed, but I never heard the sound of her laughter. It was as though her spirit was enclosed in a sandal-wood box, fragrant of another life in another land. She had been married, as I knew from other friends, to a kind and good-natured, but nervous and melancholy man, and I inferred in her a resolute and determined self-control. It was only over the tiniest flaws in the esthetic appointment of her rooms, a flower faded or misplaced in a vase, that I ever saw her for a moment show distress.

To this rule of deliberate composure, absolute in her life—perfectly expressed by the fine lines of her face and stature, all strength and grace—she possibly owed her salvation; perhaps there was no illness or unhappiness for her but in failure to abide by it. Certainly there are those, we both knew such, who create for themselves a positive need of suffering, and who scarcely feel that they really exist

save in distress. And this brings me back to the
friends of whom I have spoken. With Paul Bourget
Edith had a great literary friendship; she enjoyed,
as we all did, his brilliant and paradoxical talk, so
widely ranging, so charged with thought and feeling, where the freest of opinions and the stiffest of
theories perpetually clashed. She used to say, as
many others said who knew him, that his talk was
better than his novels, into which he never put the
whole of himself. For Minnie Bourget she felt
great tenderness, even compassion; she felt that
Bourget, delighting as he did in his wife's exag-
gerated sensibility, induced in her, as by con-
tagion, a morbid and abnormal condition. 'It's all
his fault,' said Edith severely. The slightest ailment,
five minutes' delay in her return home at the usual
time, threw him into a fever of agitation that he
never attempted to conceal. She was thus surrounded by an atmosphere of disquiet and uncertainty that was obviously made to destroy all self-
reliance. The sweetness of her nature, her single
and absorbing love for her husband, matching his
own for her, weakened every effort in her to resist
her fate. Bourget's fears for her were but too well
grounded, and Edith's severity, her censure of his
uncontrolled anxiety, but too well justified in the
end. But I need not here relate how Minnie in
her exquisite languor slipped into illness, and from
illness to death.

If I have dwelt on the case of these friends and
their hapless consent to morbid influences—so
strangely united in him with the strictness of his
theories and the brilliance of his talk—it is because

Edith was or appeared to be so complete a contrast. She seemed to keep the four main channels of her life—her writing, her friendships, her care for beauty in her surroundings, her royal and attentive charities—as distinct, as purposefully directed for the refreshment of her being, as though they were the waterpipes of her beloved garden. Hours of drought there might be—at times I suspected that there were; but then she simply disappeared with a word—'I'm so tired.' It was the only hint that beneath the even surface there was another and a hidden existence.

For me the wonder was that within this armature of her exacting taste she could pursue a literary task so remote from her daily life amongst us. I never knew her return to the United States, and she seemed in her books to treat her compatriots with severity, charming and interesting as were all those whom I met in her company. And yet she seemed able to retain her impression of the world she had left and to keep it as vivid as though she had never left it—as though she woke every morning in the heart of New York, with all its pulses beating around her. Such is of course the gift of imagination, and my surprise would have been ingenuous but for her apparent 'alibi' in our midst, so complete that she seemed to belong nowhere else. 'Where *is* she really, in spirit,' I used to ask myself as I watched her, 'here or over there?' She seemed entirely at home with us, talking her perfect French in that level voice, in that charming drawing-room of hers, with its *chinoiseries* and its wealth of flowers—was it really hers, or had it come to her, just as it was, as a gift from the hands of the Demoiselles Colombe of old days to a novelist from across the ocean? Certainly it was a far cry from that *Hudson River Bracketed* that I so much admired. I loved her too well to read her objectively; I was always trying, as I read, to analyse the working of her invention. How much of it all was experience, how much observation, memory, imagination? That extraordinary figure, for example, quite unimaginable over here, of the corpulent old grandmother, prophetess of the west, so shrewdly turning the spiritual profit of her hearers to her own temporal advantage—what about *her*? I was mystified by this puzzling duality in the writer, where only one side of it was ever seen in daily life.

I recall with particular pleasure the morning hours of my short visits to the Pavillon Colombe. My hostess was invisible till midday, but I thought of her as I strolled in the garden. It was her working-time, the hour of her spiritual transmigration to that other world. She wrote rapidly, I believe, after long pondering and maturing of her theme. Sometimes in the house I passed Madame Friedrich, her devoted secretary, who had just gone in to collect the morning's pages, ready for typing; I noticed the numerous sheets, the dashing script. From the garden below I watched the curtain fluttering at Edith's window, and I liked to think of the visitors who were with her up there—how she listened to their talk, pen in hand, her mind flying off to far-away scenes. And so I wandered away through the garden—or rather the gardens, for they were many: first the green parterre before the house, then the little wood, the flowery kitchen-garden, neat as a picture, the orchard with its apple-trees all in a ring, and so on to the rose-garden and its lily-pool, hummed over by bees—all of it together the creation of one will and one taste, Edith Wharton's dream come true. And presently she appeared herself, fresh and trim, her face shaded by a great straw hat, basket on arm, clippers in hand. It was the time for cutting off the roses of yesterday, whose hour was over. Make room for to-day, for the red-streaked buds all ready for the sun—clip, clip! The faded blossoms bent their necks to the scissors of fate and dropped into the basket, scattering their petals. Roses, bees, dreaming water—lilies—what a paradise!

I should have liked, as we returned to the house, to question my dear hostess about her morning's work behind the fluttering curtain. I shall never know if it was modesty, or a deliberate discretion, or simply a real need for silence and detachment; but with me at least—it may have been otherwise with her compatriots—she never lent herself to such questions. There was something in her that warded off all intrusion.

Year by year she asked me to go and stay with her at Hyères. I went once, but only once; I had—rather to her annoyance!—too many ties at home. The fact was that our lives moved in very different rhythms, as at bottom she knew. All the more I valued the friendship that she gave me. And

I think I may say that for her the circle to which I belong represented what she most appreciated in our old traditional France—the France that wears the chains of the past with pride, not as a yoke but as a bond of union.

The sight of Edith Wharton in this lucid mirror may be touched with strangeness, as I said, but there is no doubt of the speaking likeness. She advances and passes with the well-known air and movement—yet with a look, a glance in passing, that strikes me as ambiguous. The look may be answered in a moment; but as for what is familiar in the picture, I fasten with amusement on one point—that 'too much of a good thing,' as others have also found it, in the merciless perfection of her surroundings. So it tried a French eye too, the integrity *à outrance* of her taste, even as it was apt to chill the comfort of those who weren't to the classic manner born, in their looser handling of the art of life. But observe, for a different reason: not because it was a constraint in hours of ease, as when you are awed by a room too choice for careless comfort; not for this, but because it seemed to disown and deny the very backbone of its tradition, the descent that is its meaning, the natural spread of its family-tree. How instructive to find that even when we reach the same conclusion as France it is from the opposite direction, not as the members of a clan, linked each with each, but as the straying units that we are, making ourselves comfortable one by one. It is a pretty distinction, it will be granted. But what am I to make of another note in the scene, quite a new one, where strangeness becomes strange indeed? Was there ever no spontaneous gaiety, no laughter where Edith was? Frankly I am here at a loss. The same remark, curiously enough, is made to me by another French observer,* one who knew her long and well, and I can only meet it, I confess, with a stare. I am unable to imagine a company of people, be they who they may, grouped around Edith, without hearing the ring of her laughter soon resounding over the talk; she couldn't silence it in any tongue. We must here agree to differ. And she wouldn't talk about her writing? Indeed she would, with perfect freedom and simplicity, as a craftman's job, in a hundred hours that flew like minutes—but not, it is likely, when she sat down to lunch or strolled among her roses. And there may have been more than this in it at times, a wider question, as she changed the subject and evaded an expectant gaze. Did she feel the pressure of an invitation, however discreet, to hold an attitude that became her, beautiful and enigmatic, in a picture that she filled so well? If so, there might come a moment when an odd light was to be discerned in her eye, a queer and quizzical gleam. I think I saw it for an instant in the mirror.

It is the look which says, in plain English, 'No, you don't!'—an unexpected lapse into the vernacular, no doubt. It means, not less idiomatically, that if I see you composing an attitude for me, however graceful, spinning a theory about me, however obliging, and at the same time counting on my acquiescence, I shall catch you out. For why? Something as deep as life, in the English-thinking breast, ordains it. Which of us, crossing the sea (the channel or the ocean, it is all one) to land in foreign parts, has ever dropped the obstinate little

* M. Jacques-Emile Blanche, the well-known painter and writer, who died in 1942.

demon, palladium of our self-possession, that sooner or later refuses to be classed, to be placed in a category and kept there—sooner or later, and anyhow the instant our conformity is expected and assumed. It is confusing, perhaps, when an 'alibi' (happy word) is as complete as Edith's, for she might seem to have shed all her belongings, familiar sprite with the rest, in her migration; but it will never deceive those who know how easily such a settler can exchange one sky for another, wearing the style of the new climate like any native, with this consciousness at heart of being committed in the end to nothing at all. Strong in his confidence, the Anglo-Saxon stranger positively outdoes the host in the consistency of his deportment and array. It is quite natural, and Edith was well assured of her salvation. She had attained, and not without complacency she knew it, to a far closer intimacy with France than is often granted to an alien—with France of the French, the old and the traditional, which has never easily opened to a stranger's knock. But the eye of her ironic survey was quick to the mark, wherever she went, and the brisk dispatch of her humour. I don't say that she mightn't close the eye and suppress the demon at times, for a particular stroke; an English friend is entitled to recall that she could be severely and blamelessly French if thereby she could deliver upon England a neat backhander. But that was by the way: in the end there was no question where in spirit she would be found. She would be found where yourself is your own, where your authority is in your privacy, where two feet and no more are enough to stand on. I have seen the vials of her sarcasm outpoured upon many heads; I have watched, I might say felt, the sting of their precious balms; but I don't know that I have ever seen them discharged more liberally, after all, than on the claims and assumptions of that same old honourable tradition, when it is not the past that rules it with a living spirit, but convention with a dead hand.

And so that 'double life' of hers, which moved a sympathetic friend to wonder, was really less distracting than it seemed. Was her true life here or there, is it asked?—here in this ancient order, fabric of centuries, or there in the other world, the world still in the making, with which she communed in her books? It was neither here nor there, it was securely in herself, where only it could be. If she paid with a loss for the distance at which she kept the home of her birth—with a loss of much that might have been useful in her life, still more in her art—it was no loss that left her wanting any warrant from without, wherever she stood; she couldn't be less than herself, or more either, whatever her surroundings. There is one life open, only one but always open, to anybody whose law is in himself, ticking out its sanctions in one spot only, his brain. If that is how you are, then so you are, and you know it; the last word lies with yourself, and you can say it as easily among strangers as among your kin, for neither kin nor stranger can forestall it. But it doesn't follow that others are like you, or that your freedom would be good for others; authority at hand, lodged in the framework of their days, may be well for them. On this point too, I dare say, Edith's law was ready to pronounce. She liked, as every busy worker must, to see order in the world; for how but in order, how but in liberty rationally disciplined, can you think and work without exasperating loss of time? For herself she could make her own discipline, trust her for that; for others it might be right and proper that it should be imposed and maintained by prescription. Only—let there be no mistake about the nature, the dignity of the rule, the majesty of the law that is to reign. It must be the submission of the smaller, not merely to the stronger, but to the more beautiful and the more august—not to that which deadens but to that which enhances the beauty of the order it creates. Where this is seen there may be much to admire in authority—for others; and as time went on, and certain stiff old articles relaxed their hold upon her creed, she came to find beauty in a rule where perhaps she had least expected it; I think it surprised her. This is as yet to glance into the future; but let a glimpse be taken, pretty and significant, still through the same appreciative eyes.

Sometimes, through the open library-window, one caught sight of a priest stepping quickly down the path, well knowing the way, or the white *cornette* of a sister of mercy; and one understood—it was the hour of her charitable works for the poor and the children of the poor. I will not dwell on this chapter, nor speak, now that she is gone, of what she kept to herself. I only wish to say, what I knew well, that, exquisite stranger as she was, Edith Wharton went deep into our French life, to our people and the ministrants of their faith. Behind all her gardens there was still this other. She was no Catholic, and I do not think she would have called herself Protestant; we never touched on such matters. With us of the old world, especially in France, these feelings are inborn; whatever may be our attitude to the faith of our fathers, hostile or friendly, a definite attitude we have. It may be different elsewhere; I have sometimes the impression that for many Americans the question does not arise, or is resolved in a generous and far-ranging idealism. I think Edith was one of these, detesting all sectarianism, prodigal of her sympathy and help to all 'men of good will,' capable of the utmost self-devotion in case of need. Almost my last glimpse of the Pavillon Colombe came in a photograph she sent me of a scene under the trees—a procession, the canopy borne by the priests, the girls with their white veils, the good little boys, the sisters of mercy, the children with their baskets on their necks, scattering flowers before the Host: the *Fête-Dieu* of France, in her garden.

XII

Sainte-Claire le Château

Meanwhile much was happening elsewhere; things were doing in the south of which already a hint has been caught. That other garden of paradise, those hill-terraces with their obedient hyacinths, it is time to hear more of these. It was not so very long, a year but barely two, after the Pavilion had been called into new being that I saw for myself what had happened in the south. Rumour and report had naturally not been wanting. Even before tackling the Pavilion, as soon as ever the war-shadow was lifted, she had slipped off to the south for a winter of content—to the blessed light of the olive-land, the classic shore, the Roman Province; and there, settling in the town of Hyères, she had recovered the peace of old days in exploring the beauty of the land with the most congenial of companions; and thither again, the Pavilion achieved, she had returned in another flight as undeviating as a swallow's—and this time, it would seem, with a definite design, for where would she ever return for second thoughts and further re-searches but with a definite design? Anyhow this time she did more than explore—she pounced. Just above the old town of Hyères, on a terrace backed by the hoary *maquis* that climbed away to a ruined castle on the hilltop, stood a house, low and grey, flanked by two squat towers—Sainte-Claire le Château, once a nunnery of Poor Clares, now empty and uncared-for, but compact in its sturdy worth: the house for her, if she wished for a winter-home in utter contrast to the discreet little mansion of the north and its bowery garden. If you there looked back to a century of polite behaviour, from the rocky hillside of Provence it was an age that opened, through a vista of old rough history, broadening away to the great bowl of the midland sea, brimmed with light— to Rome, to the Grecian isles, to Carthage and Tyre, as far as you please, till sight was lost. Here indeed was enough for enticing rumour. And at last to see her on the flagged terrace, between its two pollarded planes, draw-ing her guest into more charming rooms, among still more abundant flowers, was really to rub one's eyes; for where had she been seen a moment ago but in the house of her desire, the dream come true?—and now here she was again, still housed in a dream, but in a different world. Well, it was as real as the other; the wand had been waved, the spell had worked, the thing was done. She cried out at the notion of the waving of a wand— there had been a great deal more to it than that, in this as in the other dreamwork; she wondered at herself to think of it. And she might indeed, for what she had made was not only another house and garden, it was a new winter and spring for every year, to last her to the end.

It had been perfect planning, needless to say. Sainte-Claire, when its turn came round with the fall of the year, received the daily life of the Pavilion, just as it was, without ruffling a feather of its adornment; and on it went as usual, but only with a larger light and air in which to spread its range. Hyères was the very place for it. There was already, or there was very shortly, a gathering of friends in the offing; Paul Bourget and his wife had long been winter-settlers at Costebelle, near by, and others, few and fit, soon joined the cluster. And a great point was that this fragrant and lovely country-side was France, was the bowl of the Mediterranean, was the boon southern air—and yet it was not, it was worlds away from being, the mere common toy-show of the Riviera; Edith was firm on the distinction, though there was no harm in the fact that the playthings were round the corner, close at hand, if ever a drop from the nobler pitch was desirable. From near and far she could help herself to good company, and her guest-rooms, multiplying apace, had their fill. All this could be foreseen; what was newer and more original was the custom that grew up at once and settled down, the habit of a choice little Christmas house-party, punctual to the season—original I call it for the homely sound, a novel note in the feasts of Edith's year. It soon became a dear little tradition, quite a family affair; and a family that you choose for yourself, not accept as it comes or as you find it, was clearly the sort for her. It was a small party, gathered about a nucleus of three, a triad of in-mates who upheld the tradition throughout the days of Sainte-Claire. G. L. was himself, I may surely say, the solidest pillar of the occasion, the most deeply grounded in old times; when he and Edith get together over the freemasonry of their American past it is the talk of initiates, arch and pregnant, and simple ears may make what they can of it. John Hugh-Smith for the next, not easily to be excluded from their mysteries, for he insists on knowing all about them, all about everything; and his mingled stream of ideas the readiest, curiosity the greediest, and chuckling derision the most comfortable, flows where it will. And then for the third—but the third of this essential knot, he more identified than any with the life of Sainte-Claire, still remains to be seen, and his memory to be invoked; it is memory now, and no more.

He, Robert Norton, was associated from the first with the discovery and invention of Sainte-Claire, and the whole story of the place was threaded through, to the end, with the pleasant amenity of his presence. He came and went, came again or roamed near by, till at last he was left alone in the country that he loved, in the home he had made for himself by the neighbouring sea. It is indeed through his report, given me a short while before his death, that I chiefly see the picture of those winters and springs, that southern half of Edith's later life. It is a picture seen through the eyes of a sensitive and accomplished artist, tracking his delight in the beauty of the world where it led him, with the lean vigour of one who moved unencumbered and travelled light through the world of his choice: a quick-eyed amateur, glancing and roving, drinking deep of the fresh air of his freedom. He was at home with his attractive work in the field, under changing skies; and then he was at home in all company, quietly alert, slipping into his place with courteous and habitual ease; and then again, detaching himself, he was away to the open, with a gracility of the wild that was in him, tense and lithe beneath his civilised well-being. At home or abroad, indoors or out, he was a good companion, very good for Edith. He knew the world as a member of it, secure in his place as in his freedom, and both his freedom and his place were English of the English sort, involving neither argument nor defence. As for his company out of doors, it liberated her deep-welling love of the country; it was natural, roaming and rambling with him, to look around, look away and without, with straight eyes and contented mind; and as for his place in the English world, it was something she appreciated and respected—perhaps with a touch of envy for the tranquillity of its assurance. He came from a substance of English life, school and profession and public service, of which she knew nothing to speak of; and the contact, through him, with that calm story could have its value. This was one at any rate who enjoyed the society of the world and didn't fear solitude; and his presence, I can well imagine, might quiet the restlessness haunting a mind that isn't sure of its serenity in the company of itself.

Here was the friend with whom she could really enjoy the lovely land; he helped and never hindered enjoyment. They talked long and happily as they pursued their discoveries, day after day, in those early months of leisure and liberation; talk with Norton was a voyage on smooth seas, with time and room in plenty for appreciation and amusement. He sat with her in the car, till even the patient car refused the tasks she set it; she walked with him—she was always a light-footed walker on an unknown trail. They scrambled, they lost their way, they were possibly benighted—nothing mattered in such a cause; with Norton she could even allow the country its own freedom, as he did, and follow its moods. Or on a fine spring evening, on a hillside overlooking a lonely bay, while he sat and drew, she could watch and wait near by as the scene shaped itself into a poem, an impression of peace in words to match his painting. Did anyone say she was not a true countrywoman? If so, it was the same old trouble: she was fastened to a part that others had chosen for her, not she. Henry James himself, she laughed to remember, had long ago done so, taking no denial. He couldn't have her a country-lover, it was a false note in the consistency of her case as he saw it; she had 'tasted too much blood,' he forcibly put it, to be content with the mere milk of rusticity. Well, that is the comfort of the easy-going Englishman—he holds you to nothing; on the whole he assumes that you share the tastes of an easy-going Englishman, and thinks it only natural that you should. Norton, to be sure, had his own flash of insight in his clear dark eye; he knew her well, nor her alone—he knew the sex (here is Henry again) 'so unnaturally termed the gentler'; but he was entirely of his race in his serene inclination to leave well alone and to let you be. Anyhow there she was, as she always said she was, happy in the country—not by herself, never that, but with another whose mind was akin. And at length, when the house of Sainte-Claire was finished and its guest-rooms filled, her country-life had taken its form and was ready for others to share as they came.

Tastes may differ concerning a day in the country, how it should be designed for pleasure; but on one point there could be no disagreeing when Edith led. Everyone must prefer, in sunshine and fair weather, a meal in the aromatic open, among myrtle and lentisk, to sitting at a table under a ceiling; they must indeed. Some there may have been who felt that her passion for a picnic was excessive; but she didn't stay to argue. In good time the party is packed into the car, with all the right equipment, complete in every detail—all except the essential stick or cloak, map or book, that has been forgotten as usual, that is remembered as we start: do we ever get as far as the gate without a flurry and a halt? And here it is, all the

time, just where it should be; her faithful ministers are
never at fault, if only she could ever quite believe it.
('Have you remembered the anklets against the bites of
sharks?' asked one of the party anxiously—he called her
the White Knight.) Out, then, to the olive-sprinkled
hillside, the wide slopes cushioned with the green domes
of the umbrella-pines, the sparkling sea-plain. If you sit
in the corner of the car and look about you gingerly, as
though you liked the landscape in moderation, in its
proper place, keeping its bounds, she notes and scorns
you; but if you do, don't be afraid—she is too old a traveller to think that travel should or need be discomfort. If
there is one thing on which she prides herself it is her
unerring eye for a picnic-place, the perfect spot as it
appears; and there it is. Next, and now all may help, to
find the tree, the mound, the gentle slope that provides
a 'back' for Edith, facing aright, with its due of sun and
shade. That found, and Edith settled, the strapped
hampers (which she likes to think of as 'corded bales')
are set by her side, the rugs spread, the guests 'star-
scattered' in their places: poetic allusion is never amiss
at these symposia. Nobody at this point is to help her;
she unpacks, distributes, apportions all. Nor will you
find that anything lacks of the meal you might have
enjoyed indoors, save the ceiling and the table. And
here, as Thackeray might say, a very pretty game may
be played—each reader of these lines choosing what he
would like best for lunch and imagining it produced from
the hampers. He will not go far wrong. It is a well-
furnished scene in the best tradition; it reminds me of
Pickwick for its hearty abundance, of the Lake Poets
for its seemly rurality, and of whom shall we say?—of
Alice once more, for the irresponsible dance of its

laughter. For I repeat—we are not afraid of literature here, nor of nonsense either; and in a mingling of both the long chain of Edith's picnics, under so many a sky, stretches back into the distance.

She might rest in the landscape for an hour of poetry or mirth; she wasn't answerable for the ways of nature. Her garden was another matter; for her garden was the nursery of her own young charges, that were always on her mind, and those of Sainte-Claire were a wilder brood, in spite of the example of the hyacinths, than the orderly bevies of the Pavilion. They gave more trouble from the beginning, and they might for that very reason be nearer to her heart. She was a kind wise parent—not as playful or indulgent as some, but she planned untiringly for the young things' higher good. The tangled wilderness, that at first lacked even the soil for their nourishment, was soon blossoming in a score of nooks, sheltered clefts, friendly little enclosures, enhancing as by accident its negligent charm. She made her rounds with the gardener at all hours, earnest in consultation; nothing happened but at her word and by her will. Discipline, as ever, was strict; she would have no shirking or sulking, and it was a stupid little plant that ever dreamed of dodging her eye. But it was a fine life for honest effort; liberty, so you know how to use it, was the note of the garden, adventure when you have learnt control. The only possible complaint might have been that she never seemed to find the leisure to be cosy and comfortable and confidential with her brood; there were no jolly times when they had her all to themselves, out of working hours; when the day's exercises were over it was the end of the day. It might appear as though something were wanting: was she really *fond* of her garden, for all her delight in its gallant growth, her pride in its success, her pleasure in its bright young looks? It could be doubted; she was so very judicious, so vigilant in her care for its deportment. Yet there came a time, as her friends remember, when she was seen as Rachel, refusing to be comforted. A cruel month of frost, the worst of a century, had fallen upon the garden at the height of its prospering career, laid it waste and cut off whole legions of these promising young lives. She was inconsolable, it even made her seriously ill. If this was not love indeed, who ever loved a garden?

The ruins were repaired, the ranks replenished, but there were lasting scars—on the heart of the gardener, it may be, as well as on the stricken field. Enough of that. In other and happier seasons there were interested visitors of all degrees, to whom the garden was shown off in its bloom—from the true master of the art and craft, whose word of appreciation is a prize, to the choric enthusiasts whom we all know, with their chanting tongues and wandering eyes, hymning your paradise with their thoughts upon their own, to seize a clever hint, to draw a complacent contrast. These let us wish away, and turn for better amusement to another friend and guest, one in particular, whose abounding good will was only equalled by her capacious ignorance, not of gardens alone, but of the whole realm of nature in flower and leaf: Edith's well-loved sister-in-law from New York, a yearly visitor, inexhaustible in zest and humour and discourse. It was as good as a play, an extravaganza of the lightest, when Mrs. Jones took the place in hand for examination. Her discoveries were beyond prediction. It was she, according to legend, who returned from an autumnal stroll in the country with the lamentable news of the many fine trees that were dying or dead, their leaves positively falling in showers, withered and brown: could nothing be done to save them? That story must have been true. At any rate it is certain that she stepped out onto the terrace of Sainte-Claire, on a May morning, announcing her intention to inspect and report on the whole domain for the benefit of her daughter, a distinguished garden-architect, to whom she would render an exact account of all that was in flower. 'What will you say are these, to begin with?' asked Edith, pointing to the line of tall rose-coloured tulips that edged the terrace. That was easy—'Why, poppies, of course,' cried Mrs. Jones promptly. She was a visitor in a thousand, for any gardener, with these flowers of surprise blooming at every turn. She had such a knowledgeable air as she rushed her enquiries, such a sapient twinkle as she delivered her view, such a large good-humour in the exposure of her rashness—she was irresistible. Edith followed her round with joy. In the chequered life of a gardener it is a green and gushing hour, relaxing care, that is passed in the garden with Minnie Jones.

Edith, it strikes me, took the same line with the books in her library as with the plants out of doors. No doubt the ways of true love are many with both, and her way with books was that of a lover indeed, but of a lover by no means tender to caprice. Her books were all around her in the house, they had the run of the place from floor to floor, she couldn't exist without them; but her rule was sovereign still. They too were not to expect that she would dawdle about with them at odd hours; there was no subsiding over a book at haphazard, in the first armchair. No, but at bedtime, or whenever she went to rest, she clasped her book, the newest, the latest on the table, where the inflowing stream made its fresh deposit almost daily. Sometimes it was thought that the book had a scared look as she carried it off, as though it knew what it was in for; but a brave book appreciates a sporting encounter, standing up to such a reader, with such a challenge to prove its mettle, and we needn't pity it. But then what happens? The book, when it is seen again, has evidently had a tough time of it, whatever the result; but has it actually had fair dealing? For a book, once taken in hand, reasonably asks to be read, and it hardly seemed believable that she could really have read it. Some denied that she had ever read it; it wasn't humanly possible, they said, that she could have covered the ground in the time. Some even put it more coarsely: she called it reading, but it was violating, gutting, savaging a book, to use it as she did. Yet it was never easy to convict her of a too hasty dispatch; she could give an account of her judgment, clearly reasoned, firmly founded, as you soon learn if you begin to dispute it. What then is the use of patiently plodding at your reading, as some of us do, if you are no better furnished in the end than Edith by her lightning assault? I don't know: and yet the luxurious turning of page by page, the surrender, not meanly abject, but deliberate and cautious, with your wits about you, as you deliver yourself into the keeping of the book for all the time it takes—isn't this the true felicity of a lover of books? This I call reading, and if this is reading I certainly don't think Edith often read.

But there is another chance for a book of the right kind, and that is when it is read aloud in the right company, on winter evenings, with Edith for once quiescent in her sofa-corner, watching the gradual projection of the book upon the listening air. This is quite a new picture—I never heard of such a thing in other years; it must have been the influence of the family party that was still at its genial work. Anyhow a book was opened, I think generally in the hand of Norton, a fine reader— an approved book, a novel of ripe years, to be drawn out in its fulness by due degrees, night after night. It is the right way with the right book; so it grows in smooth and steady liberation, and not the reader only, but the listeners in their circle help to fashion it in their united attention. It is all very well, but is it possible to believe that Edith would stay in her corner, waiting on the pace of the story, keeping time with the rest? She certainly loved these sessions, she jealously guarded them from intrusion; but the party was often at a loss, no doubt, to save the book. For the great masters, especially of our tongue, are not to be hustled in the enjoyment of their freedom; if you wish for their society you must suffer their manners, once for all, careless or unruly as you find them. And that was the trouble with Edith; the misdeeds of the masters were so shocking to her that she couldn't pass them or put up with them for a moment—not from overniceness, rather from a sort of rage at their perversity, their want of conscience in their play. Some of them had to be quite excluded, if the evening was to end happily; Scott could never be admitted, nor Dickens either, incorrigible monsters; there was no more to be said—she saw only their crimes. Thackeray, with his limber ease, the sweep of his flexible wrist, the tunable charm of his speech, could be indulged for a time, supreme while it lasted, till he too was in disgrace for his sentimental frailties. It looks as though it would be hard to find the great work of a great master that would hold its own: are there any who are beyond reproof? Everybody on the spot names one—Jane Austen of course, wise in her neatness, trim in her sedateness; she never fails, but there are few or none like her. There is George Eliot indeed, who may have her faults, but even Edith, for old sake's sake, as in filial tenderness, could be blind to these—righting the balance by a curt dismissal of Charlotte Brontë, with her great baleful eyes. So the quest proceeds, with varying fortune, and it may be best in the end to turn to some sound entertainer, not of the highest pretension, of whom all isn't asked and who wins by giving more than is expected. Edith could always settle back in her corner, comfortable and approving, to attend, if you please, to the ambling chronicles of Trollope. I don't blame her for that; and yet, where Mannering, Copperfield, Newcome have been rejected, I may resent seeing the floor cleared for Phineas Finn. It is a question of propriety, if no more. However, anything for an evening of straight reading, and a book to be created anew, chapter upon chapter, from start to finish.

There were evenings of poetry too, and out of these there grew another book in course of time, after a different fashion—an anthology, as was only natural; for where listeners in a harmonious circle begin to call for the poems of their choice—still calling upon Norton, a reader to be trusted with the choicest—it is clear that a lyrical garland is gradually created, displaying the unity of the circle itself. Linked in this affinity, the poems cling together by a law of their being, and together let them remain in a printed book. So the anthology is rounded, and it surely speaks a volume for the concord of the circle if it is a collection of the most intimate kind, poems of the inspiration that every mortal shares, and yet it is the unique possession of every mortal. The best and the very best of English love-poetry: if it is possible to bring such a matter before a conclave, that will deliberate in a ring and elect by acclamation, this is a fellowship indeed. It is a delicate scrutiny to be conducted in concert, and a sensitive appraisal for the voices of so many, few though they were. But there was no embarrassment for this happy band in their sessions, as they faced each other over an exquisite research. They began from its height; for where is the diapason of truth and beauty to be heard in the speech of a lover, if not in the utterance of Roman Antony and the 'lass unparallel'd'?—and nothing was to be approved but whatever rang true in its kind to their immortal music. Nor is it a research where the way is plainly marked by the great poetic names; on the contrary, when you have left Shakespeare the way seems rather to avoid the greatest and to wind deviously among the lesser—many of whom, looking in their hearts, are translated above the highest for their hour, while they speak to all attending ears. It is with the singers of love as with the birds in May; lordlier fowl are silent when the large-eyed nightingale is awake. Of the circle of listeners at this moment I have only to look at one, and I easily see her. She sat there in her corner, all alight and aglow, feasting on the music, with a bravery of joy in which there was neither doubt nor shade of reluctance. Life with this beauty in it is life to be trusted after all; the rest is forgotten. The anthology of the poems of love, when it appeared, was a slender volume, and as with other anthologies everyone will add to it and take away from it in the reading; but there was much pleasure in the making for these few.

But if we talk of books in the making, what about the books that were made upstairs, day by day, in the sacred hours of the morning—behind the window-curtain that perpetually stirred, here as at the Pavilion, with the wind of the ghostly visitors from afar? They were as urgent as ever. The unwritten books still way-laid her in every corner; and her eye lit up as 'what a subject!' she exclaimed—all her companions knew that cry. Very often it meant that the book she was writing must be dropped for a dash to be made at another—at an opening chapter, a crucial scene, to pacify the in-truder. Who spoke of failing material, in the rootless con-dition of her life?—here was her answer, her hands were always full to overflowing. But there was no fear for the book she was writing; she turned back to it and away it went, prompt off the mark. Three stages she dis-tinguished in its course, regular in their succession. First the blithe beginning, with all its promise in the air, exhilarating as a ride through a green forest; it is a lovely book, lovelier than any, the book of those first chapters, dancing ahead of you in the freshness of its release. Then indeed, and before long, the landscape changes; there is that arduous middle tract, where the book must be overtaken, checked, controlled, for strict concentration on its purpose. It is no spring forest now, it is a desert plain and a trudge in deep sand. Here was the time when she might be glad to talk things over, if there was a hitch or a snag in the track—when she would carry the pages of the morning downstairs and read them to her friends, demanding their counsel. They listened with drawn brows, severely attentive; unsparing opinions were asked and declared. It she didn't take their advice the talk still cleared the way; nothing composes and confirms the mind like advice that you meet and resist. And so to the book again for the third stage of the journey, the straightest of all, when with everything in order, each call foreseen, you approach the final descent—faster and faster, till you find yourself, as she liked to say, 'tobogganing' to the end. That is how a book is written if that is how you can write a book; and she could, and she did it a dozen times. 'Don't take your book too hard,' she says, if she sees you breaking your head over your own. If it won't respond, won't look up and wave to you in its enjoyable course, it is that you don't *know* your book, haven't closed with it and mastered its confidence. Well, she knew *her* book at any rate; she knew how it took the subject, exposed, developed, revolved it to the close. In short she had her 'method' in the hollow of her palm, and had had it there by now for so long that the book in the brain was forthwith the book on the paper, with no scars or marks of struggle in the process. Hard work is happy work when hand and brain keep time so nicely. It might have been the better for her book if there had been more tension, less composure between the two; but it couldn't have worn a more shining face.

And to complete the picture and to round off the record of the *acta diurna* of Sainte-Claire, here is another note that should not be forgotten, a new one again. It is the note of music—to a rippling accompaniment of surprise on the part of all who knew her, including herself; for none could remember the time, till quite lately, when music had not been completely dumb to her, and she had ignored it as a thing that was no concern of hers, having nothing to say. But now it appeared that music would speak after all if she listened, and she was immensely pleased, for a time quite excited, by the discovery of its unsuspected voice. She went to concerts, there was music in her house, she even acquired a gramophone with a copious repertory. The musical among her friends were called to join her—not that she looked for their advice or guidance, for as usual she knew her own way to what she needed; but she liked to listen in good company. 'I don't think she was really musical,' says one of the company *—'the taste came to her as a sort of intellectual graft.' Certainly it was a pleasure to her intelligence, this new field in which to discriminate and to judge; and at times, if you watched her distributing her opinions, speaking up and talking back, so to say, to Bach or to Mozart, to Beethoven or to Wagner, it did appear as though she might have been shyer of them if her feelings had been as sensitive in their presence as her wits were alert. It may seem absurd, but I am reminded, by its contrast, of another sight of her, an impression of a moment. I never but once saw her seated herself at the piano; as a girl, I believe, she had practiced her scales and played her piece like the rest, but she had long forgotten any familiarity she ever had with the keyboard; and she now sat at the piano as if it were a strange and utterly mysterious machine, and she touched the keys as if she hardly knew what would happen next; but she found the notes she wanted, the three notes of the chord of C major, and her expression was positively beatific as they chimed together, 'not a fourth sound but a star.' Harmony, heavenly harmony— it spoke and she heard: 'How *lovely!*' she cried. The reader, as I say, may smile; and yet, when I see her listening to a symphony or a sonata, and when at the

* Mrs. Winthrop Chanler.

[191]

close it is admired or damned so promptly, and when Schubert or Schumann are extolled or rebuked so decidedly—not, I must say, with any technical pretension, but with no room for doubt—then I recall that chord of C major, and the look of her delight as she softly struck it; and there seems to be more music in that moment than in all the rest of the concert. But whatever it was, music indeed, or the interest of discovering that it possessed a voice of its own after all, she had found something new.

Such were the works and days of Sainte-Claire in those good times; and good they were, for Edith was never shy of happiness when it came—she took it with a sincerity that was frank and wholesome. She was no friend to the distemperature that frowns on happiness, when you can have it, as a slur upon the dignity of woe— that dolorous feint of pride at bay. She would have no nonsense in her life, no airs or flourishes of resignation; but more than this, there was a spring of enjoyment in her that never sank or slackened. 'I am born happy every morning,' she said, and it was true enough; the blue of the morning was always clear in her vision. She never grew tired of the number of things in the world. Sainte-Claire, one of the best of them, was still more plastic under her hand than all the rest. It was inexhaustible; the house grew, the garden spread, the domain itself went pushing up the hillside, among the warm grey rocks and the sweet grey herbage, till it reached and embraced the old ruined castle at the top, where it watched over the level of the plain, the green miles stretching away to the rim of the sea. It was a fair ground. There was solace in that air, where winter may freeze but scarcely shows itself to the eye—where cypress and ilex, olive and juniper, know no seasons; and there was revival in it too, where spring breaks through the heart of winter, and a new flower opens in the garden whenever you look for it. And if there was a good omen and a favouring influence that hung about the place, it was assigned, Edith liked to assign it, to an association that it happened to possess. It was a likely touch of chance that had bestowed it. Follow the driveway from the house, where it coils beneath the terrace of the tulips, and you come to a small, perhaps an unbeautiful cottage that stands by the gate; going out or coming in, you may glance at it with interest. Edith was pleased to add that cottage to her possessions. It was a common thing to look at, flimsy and trivial, but it was 'La Solitude'—if memory is stirred by the name. 'I was only happy once,' wrote Robert Louis Stevenson before his death, 'that was at Hyères'; and 'La Solitude' was where he had happily lived and worked—not for long, but it stayed in his remembrance in that light. Edith's departing guest, turning out of the gate into the highroad at Hyères, left the ghost of Stevenson, who was happy there, still in friendly occupation.

XIII

Past and present

To have old friends round you wherever you stay, to find new wherever you go, to take your choice of the best in several lands and languages—it is a great fortune, and I look nowhere over her life without seeing her in possession of it. Her devoted companions, her ardent admirers, vie with each other in the refinement of their tribute, recounting the manifold reward of her friendship. A great fortune: and yet, as I watch her enjoying it, I am moved to wish for her at times, what she never had nor apparently missed, some measure of the grateful shade that is open to most of us, that freedom of retirement from the opinion of those about us—the timely refuge of their indifference. This retreat, I see too well, was never granted her, and indeed she might have felt it an unsuitable eclipse; at any rate she did nothing to secure it. I am not now thinking of the outlying regions, we know they existed, where it was another kind of attention that she faced—the fringes of her magnetic field where the law of her attraction was reversed. It is true that to the last there were spots where she aroused, not unwittingly, a bristle of hostility as little to be wondered at as denied; but let it pass. It injured none; it was the sharp shock that enlivens the clack of tongues, not wounds in silence. But was there nothing else in her exposure that might appeal for some slackening of the regard, some slight blurring of the appreciation, bent on her from closer quarters, even the closest? Watch her where admiration and affection alone surround her, and still you see that she was not of those on whom mercy falls unstrained. I hardly know how it is, but her praises are a paean that is not the loose warble of indulgence. She didn't ask for that? Very likely: but it is not only for the asking that it is given to others—to those whose very faults are cherished because with all their faults they are 'like themselves.' Such are they, figures and characters, who strike true to the note and punctual to the hour of their own peculiarity, whatever it may be. And such was not Edith; she with her faults, whatever they were, did not illustrate and affirm, she contradicted herself—unreasonable who was the soul of reason, unjust who was the champion of fair play. I have glanced at this embroilment before, and I do so again for one moment; for it points and heightens the pleasure of meeting the large army that now advances. There is no restriction or scruple in the homage of this whole-hearted throng; and here they are.

But first a concourse not to be discerned in detail, without faces to be distinguished. There is neither count nor track to be kept of these; they are all who looked to her for help and all whom she helped in need. 'I cannot remember her ever refusing an appeal to her charity,' says Robert Norton, speaking of knowledge,

once she was satisfied of its own good faith. And not only of money, but of time and thought she was equally unsparing. Often it happened that distant friends, sure of their ground, would recommend some protégé to her care; and she would find herself responsible for a series of lame ducks, totally unknown or without claim on her, to whom she gave the same ungrudging care as to the rest. And not only time and money and thought, but personal sympathy and interest. I can recall case after case of lives that she helped to brighten and straighten out. Her war-work and the charities arising from it are well known—her efforts for big causes such as the Fondation Foch, and her annual bazaar in Paris on behalf of a curé in the *"zone rouge"* of the outer city, who was putting up a single-handed fight against atheism and anarchy and making headway. Of the day-to-day appeals for relief and her response I should have known nothing, but for my yearly visits to Sainte-Claire. She never lost touch with the cases she helped, and welcomed letters from anyone she had befriended.

And G. L.:

She was possessed by a sense of compassion deeper and more authentic than I have ever seen in any other human being. I call it authentic because, as I observed it in action, it was independent of any theory of justice or any personal interest. The knowledge that there was mitigable suffering in the life of a particular man or beast was enough to unseal the spring of her pity; and she was ready to submit to boredom and to something near disgust if she was assured that she herself and not merely material relief was what was needed. I have seen

[196]

many instances of this, and what she did she did
nobly and tenderly—those nearest to her knew best
at what cost.

Such was her charity: no principle of benevolence, no
mission of duty or service, but an impulse of her being
to which all her intelligence and all her imagination
joined their strength. She was as little a professional
philanthropist as she was a devotee of humanity; yet
the good that she did had the virtue of both, in careful
consideration, in vivid insight. Moreover there blew
through it all a fresh and animating air, a breeze of good
sense and good fellowship, that lent a rare grace of its
own to her liberality—till it seemed the most natural
thing in the world for help to be given and taken
wherever it availed, and no more ceremony to it than
that. No one who knew Edith Wharton knew her more
easily, simply, directly than those to whom she held
out the light and steady hand of her beneficence. She
left them feeling that they, more than any, really knew
her as she really was, and they may well be right.

Between these and Edith I do not care to intervene with more words; they are together in their understanding. But of those who next appear it is easier speaking. They are her friends of a younger and much younger
age than her own, of whom later years brought many;
and again there is only one voice here—she was an en-
chanting friend to youth. Once more it was the lightness
and airiness of her alliance with these newcomers, as
she talked and laughed with them, that was the sign of
its charm. She met them as they came, they came to
meet her; she made no arrangement of her welcome to
the young, no preparation of her ease in greeting them,

and they joined hands in a moment. So many indeed were the agreeable contacts that she made of this kind, across a deepening gap of years, that she must have had a special gift and talent in the matter—and not one of the most likely, as it might seem, to be hers; for what had then become of her memorable shyness, which might well have wrought formidably in her dealing with youth? What *is* the gift, wherever it is seen at work? It is certainly not that of an everlasting juvenility, evading the due and seemly touch of time; to be false to your station and degree in age is no way to partnership with true youth. It is another and a sounder grace that is needed—the power of acquiring your age without dropping your youth, of discovering how it is to be old without losing what it was to be young. If your years, piling their seasonable rings, still enclose the living stuff of your past, there are mistakes that you will not make. You know that to be young or old, if that is all, is no happier, no sweeter, no braver than to be old or young; you know that there is no category of old or young, for a distinction of character or kind; you know in short that old or young is human, whatever the mark of its humanity. In this clearance of the air you find no need to be fearful or mistrustful of youth, none to oppose it and none to flatter it; and there, if you like, is ground for a genuine compact. What may then astonish you is that youth should see strangeness in age, as though time could make changes in kind. And pleasing and perhaps touching it is to you when youth discovers the error with surprise—best of all with frank and outspoken satisfaction. That, then, is the secret—to remain what you have been in becoming what you are; and Edith was one who had so remained.

As for her shyness, with all the interpretations that have been placed on it, let us here speak of it for the last time; in the company now present it is seen no more. The gap of years, though it was bridged so easily that it seemed to be abolished, had that good effect—and very naturally too, for years are a protection of nature, and much better than any of defensive art. When you have time and its resources, time and its reassuring authority to take care of you, your old uneasy armature may be put off with relief. The use of it was to guard your privacy and to save your confidence from surprise, and both are safe enough when time is on your side. True, there are forward and malapert young people as well as old—some say there are more; but Edith at any rate could have no difficulty with these, by a turn of the wrist she could dispose of them; if any had the face to encroach unduly, I am sorry for them. But is there really that excess of eagerness in the siege of their elders by the young—and isn't it rather a fact that most of us, ensconced in our years, would not unwillingly see more of it? On the whole, we may feel, it seems hidden from youth that its addresses and attentions, even its familiarities, will not be misprized. That, however, was no concern for Edith; there were no invaders, the freshest or the brightest, for whom she had to wait. And while she took them as they came, now one and now another, not as a company or a generality but as singular friends, no doubt but she saw one attraction in them all alike— her own youth, her young curiosity and avidity, her young ambitions and aspirations; she knew what these were, and the kind of satisfaction that had been sweet to them—nobody knew better than she. The things she had wanted were now the things she had to give—the good things, which she didn't affect to disparage, that accrue by the fortune of years. So let the young people approach and see for themselves what she is, the rare creature of whom they have heard so much. There she is, sitting very upright and straight-backed, but all alive, easy and active in repose: it is a pleasing echo that I catch as I write from a young observer in the past. He of the present, I should hope, is bolder in his advance than that other; but perhaps it is a simpler undertaking. When Edith saw her own youth at a distance, and saw it coming to meet her in the young, it was easier approaching her than it had seemed of old.

Indeed there was something new in her expression—and perhaps more generally too, in the picture she presented, for though her years were yet light on her there was a certain loosening and softening of the sharp-cut edge of her elegance, but that was all—something new, I say, in her look as she glanced up to welcome a new generation, glanced up and caught its eye. There was a quick light of amusement and understanding, as though she knew where she was with these newcomers, needing no introduction. If they stepped up to her with spirit, so much the better; but if any faltered in doubt or diffidence—for after all everyone knew that Mrs. Wharton could be chilling if she chose—she cut short their hesitations, pulled them forward and seated them beside her with friendly decision. 'Be done with that nonsense,' she seemed to say, with attaching mockery, as though a pair of initiates, old hands so versed in the discomforts of inexperience, could easily exchange a wink. When once the countersign had passed between them, all was well and they could talk—and talk they must, the young people, to follow the fling with which she took the lead; for they couldn't hang back, she cried them on, she spurred them to keep up with her. If the shy were shaken out of their shyness, the cautious were rallied and derided; she had no patience with circumspect youth, wise out of season, still less with youth squeamish or disdainful. What's the point of youth if it doesn't see and use its great advantage, the fact that it has room to move in, time around and open to it—what's the good of it if it holds off and plays for safety in the narrower margin to which the old are confined? Wherever she saw youth making the most of its advantage she was ready to join it—not only to join it but to race and outstrip it. A delightful sight, and always delightful because there was no false touch in it whatever—none of patronage, none of condescension, none of benevolent superiority, least of all of any strain for an effect. She was equal in the fun—not equal, for she was always ahead, but it was share alike for all. And this was pleasant too, that what you saw in her as she shared the fun was not only her youth, but her youth was boyishness— there was no doubt of it. This high and intimidating lady!—but it was unmistakable, there was a frank and jolly and enterprising boy in her all the time. Girlish fancies and foibles, doubtless she knew and understood them too, but they weren't her own; she didn't encourage them, she may have enjoyed teasing them. Far more her own and more proper to her was the mixture of the whimsical and the practical, the ribald and the romantic, in the mind of a boy.

Not all, even in this brave age, are ready for talk at the pitch and pace of such a creature; and some have a dearer wish, perhaps a higher, than to race beside the admired and the distinguished—it is to sit at their feet.

I speak by the book: it is a noble exhilaration that hums in the brain of the upward-gazing acolyte. But here comes the difficulty—to know where to begin. Think, for example, of this Edith and of all that is behind her, all the experience and remembrance that is stored in a head like hers; and there it is within reach, a fascination to consider—but how do you start to broach it? What words will define a need as vague as it is vast, the need for communication at once and entirely with all that living and beckoning past, the past inside that head? I sympathise perfectly with the young friend who, overcome by the opportunities of a quiet hour with Edith as they drove together through the country, could only break out with 'O how many questions there are that I should like to ask you!' To which Edith, still with that side-look of brotherly derision in her eye, 'Well, now's your chance—ask away.' It is a poser; but Edith, reading the face of her own youth beside her, was an affable angel, and the right questions readily abounded as the answers forestalled them. To a desire that she read and recognised as the genuine thing her response was unstinted. The passion for hearing and seeing and knowing, there could be nothing she didn't recognise in that as an old familiar of her own; and the right sign on it was an absolute claim. It is the sign of a disinterested candour—all is in that. To gape for knowledge, of any kind and all of it, and only because it is enthralling as you see it—knowledge for its own sake, with no idea of adding it as a trophy to your own decoration or of sneaking experience cheaply: this is the title, the only one that is good or that is needed, to all the satisfaction you demand. Experience must be paid for and decorations must be earned; but knowledge for its own sake is free for the asking, whatever she has of it to give you. And none could know better than she the romance of it, which is the best warrant of all; for wherever there is romance it is the proof that you are outside yourself and leaving yourself behind—not an easy matter at any time of life and certainly not easiest in youth, unless with the help of romance. Here again the young votary won't find Edith aloof and withdrawn, coolly regarding him in his zeal; the magic in the air, when the hunt is up and the quarry descried, had lost none of its charm for her. This high lady once more, so distinguished for her reserve—there was always a young enthusiast in her too.

If the new friend was a writer—but here I leave the pen to one who was.

Most generous of all [writes Mrs. Gerard Goschen *] was her help to young writers. There is for me an unforgettable spring day when the sun streamed in through the window with yellow ragged tulips leaping up to meet it. Looking out I could see the waves whipped across the dark blue bay in the distance before the mistral; but in that room at Sainte-Claire all was still, and I can yet hear Edith's voice saying as she picked up my book and turned to my husband: 'But she's a born writer!' In that moment the clouds of self-distrust vanished away. I wanted to begin another book at once; nor can I ever look at ragged yellow tulips without a quick stab of stimulation.

For two years I was happy with the happiness of creative work, and when the proofs came in I wondered for the hundredth time whether I should

* Whose books are signed Vivienne de Watteville.

dare ask Edith to write a preface. It must be she or no one, I thought jealously, for it was her book, she had called it forth. When she told me to send her the proofs, I begged that she would glance through them with a red pencil. Then came days of delicious agony, days when I felt alternately that all I had written was hopelessly bad, and was steeled for her criticism—or remembered bits which said what I had wanted to say, and I felt momentarily sustained. But when her letter came, her unexpected praise sent me reeling among the stars.

And then to work. She had sent me a whole typed page of dry invaluable criticism, and granted me what every artist prays for, the opportunity to see the master at work, to be told not only 'this is bad,' but why it is bad, and how to put it right. For Edith had provided far more than a sheet of abstract criticism; she had done what not one writer in a thousand would have troubled to do, which was to go through the whole proof page by page, pencilling comments and suggestions, even correcting the punctuation.

There could be no greater sense of companionship than this going forward almost hand in hand through the pages, and nothing could have so inspired confidence. It was as though she were at my elbow; and when she had written in the margin 'rotten word' or 'I don't like this' or 'anticlimax,' she presently uplifted my drooping spirits by a generous 'good,' and when the 'good' came beside particular passages which I myself liked I could have shouted for joy. She never condemned without suggesting an alternative. Looking back through these pages I now realise how gentle she was, how careful, while condemning till one squirmed with shame, never to destroy the cobweb texture of one's confidence. In one place she had even scribbled across the page 'glorious chapter!' She was much amused in another by my perplexity over deciding which of two alternatives to keep, and wrote: 'Do step into the next aeroplane and fly over with the alternatives wrapped up in cotton wool.' When the book, with her preface, subsequently appeared, she took endless trouble to send it to England and America for review, besides giving innumerable copies to her friends.

There was romance enough in all this, romance that to a young writer means a great deal more than a helpful hand of mastery, lending its skill. It means new colour and new value for the day of work, that is lifted into a light where it takes the tinge and the dignity of heroic associations. But it was romance, as you see, that was not to lose touch with the practical; Edith's young friends, she soon let them know, weren't to bemuse themselves on dreams. Intellectual audacity as much as you please and for all you are worth: that is another matter; but the rapture of sentiment is a measured portion. It is pleasant to be caught up into a fairytale, and right to go reeling among stars at the proper moment; but from Edith you get no encouragement to waste good time. Her own taste for life, so acute in the living, was never to be distinguished (as another friend puts it) from her need for action; and you may follow the visionary gleam, but without forgetting to look where you plant your step. For a sensible dreamer she would do everything; her wits were active and stirring at once, to open the way for him and to clear it of needless obstruction. You merely waste time, she made it plain, if you won't allow a friend more luckily placed to help you; and before you could thank her she had devised her plans to help you and had carried them out, and the only thanks she desired were the works you were now free to accomplish. And what is it that wastes more time than anything else, and more hinders the right use of it, especially in the years when you should most steadily be using it aright? It is simply the want of pence, the easiest of all obstacles to be twitched aside by one who happens to have pence in hand. She scorned the superstitions that cling about money, the absurd little rites and observances, the forms of respect for its sanctity —the whole *chassé-croisé* of convention designed to solemnify a trifle. Money is a convenience, the lack of it an inconvenience, that's all—and you will kindly accept the convenience, if you need it, 'without sputterings or argument—*please!*' The tincture of gall that is distilled, none so seldom, by an obligation for money was unimaginable when the obligation was to her; for she wanted no power and claimed no authority, once you were at your proper work unhampered. We come back to it again: to owe Edith anything, her time, her trouble, her money, was to know her and to like her better than ever, and nothing less or more.

She didn't desire influence, she had no wish to take possession of your mind or to rule your faith. She wanted no followers or disciples of her own—of course not, for this would have meant precisely what she feared, a clutching of her skirts, a breach of her intimacy with herself. And besides, how easily the fresh air of intercourse, that was the breath of life to her, grows heavy and overcharged in the acting and reacting of such claims, the counterplay of feeling let loose—a stifling climate for a free spirit. But it is not to be inferred that she could refrain, safe in the open, from interference of another kind. When she saw how the people about her, and by no means only the young and inexperienced in whom it was to be expected, fumbled the ordering of their lives, muddled away their resources, bungled their plans—it was irresistible, she had to intervene and to point out what was so obvious to her, the right way to tackle their business. You might as well ask a master-craftsman to stand by in silence when he sees good material spoilt and tools clumsily handled by a novice; it is certain that the master knows best, and why pretend that he doesn't? Edith, as to what you should do, where you should go, how you should decide, whom you should (or at the least should not) admire or obey, follow or court, always knew best—and not only knew best, but knew on the stroke, at a glance: it was a rule to which none ever heard of an exception. Well, I don't say that she lightly or tactlessly intruded—nobody could impugn her taste; but you weren't in doubt how her fingers itched, or how unbearably it fidgeted her to see you embarked on the wrong task, pledged to the wrong course, charmed by the wrong person, when a word from her could set you right. 'But surely it is impossible to know enough of the affairs of others, and especially the mutual inclinations of two others, that *can* be known only to those two, to decide these things over their heads?' Yes, of course: and none was severer than she on your own hasty sentence in such matters, or clearer to decree that it must be left to men and women, stumbling or straying, cooing or squabbling, to work their own salvation. And yet— with the particular case before her the rule was still the absolute rule: she knew best. Did she really? I dare say she knew better than most, which may be no great concession; but if she didn't always know best it was because, rather surprisingly, her judgment of humanity was sounder than her judgment of human beings. Sometimes, when her advice was most trenchant, it was evident that she had failed to see far into the lives of which she was disposing. But at this point again I hand the pen to another, for a charming and penetrating note.

Edith [writes Madame de Divonne *], with all her knowledge of men and women, did not always understand them. Her divination of the depths of personality, its secret springs and hidden currents, showed so rare an insight that it was strange to find her not seldom at fault in her reading of the surface; and then she would label a character, once for all, with too positive and indelible a description. There was no gainsaying her; and though she was never tyrannical, never disposed to command or to coerce, she was often impelled to instruct—to teach you how to live. It was a part of her activity and her industry; she could not endure to see awkward or unnecessary pauses in the conduct of a life; the wheel must always be turning. And so her advice, very distinct in its terms, was promptly given if she thought you required it. Yet if it was taken, and

* Comtesse Jules de la Forest Divonne ('Claude Silve'). I am responsible for the translation of this and of a later page from the same hand.(P.L.)

good results ensued, then she drew back with exquisite delicacy, and appeared to have forgotten that she had helped you. And if her advice was rejected, she not only bore no grudge, but I have even observed in her at times, when she saw her friend take a different turning from that prescribed, a pleasant shift of mood, as though the little act of rebellion appealed to her humour. I still hear her amused laugh, over some matter on which I had gratefully listened to her counsel but had not seen my way to follow it: '*Vous souriez, vous souriez, vous remerciez—et puis vous continuez votre petit bonhomme de chemin!*' There was gaiety and real amusement in her tone, and I believe that where nothing serious was involved she was genuinely entertained by these small outbreaks of the unexpected. For with all her great gifts of creation and organisation, in her books, in the magical perfection of her surroundings, even for her there were moments of vacancy and boredom—due as often to the presence of others as to their absence; and she found a kind of relief in the occasional insubordination of her friends.

There is a ring in that laugh of amusement, so happily recalled, which is revealing to an elderly ear. Edith, it reminds me, had not only kept intact the resources of her youth, but she hadn't rejected or ever depreciated the good gifts of later age; and to both alike she could help herself at will, as they served her turn. See her, then, at a moment that is neatly caught—when younger life, smiling and grateful, slips from under her hand to make its own decision: absurd young life, as though it were capable of directing its affairs in a practical and sensible manner! Such, however, is youth; and age, if it has the wisdom and humour of Edith, turns to the enjoyment of its own advantage, one not to be despised after all—the restful privilege of age the spectator, age that is not answerable for the mistakes of the young. It is agreeable to have the confidence and companionship of youth and to be included in its play—a treat not often conceded to its elders in the measure that it was to Edith; but it is also good to sink back into the seat of the spectator, that is well placed for observing the play; and the stir of irony in detachment, quickened by the sight of the play, is justly refreshing to the brain that has deserved it. Here is a resource of which nothing can deprive a generation that has served its time; it can always look on, breathing to itself 'O you funny children!'—nor did Edith refuse that most proper and suitable entertainment on occasion. All this is the issue and result of living, as I say, continuously—never cutting yourself off from your past while always advancing into your future, gathering and collecting throughout the journey and throwing nothing away. It is the secret, not only of retaining the support of your youth, but of living on easy terms with your age; an angry and scolding age is one that, having cast out its youth, resents the loss for which it is itself to blame. With all your life still yours, the only thing that may yet seem strange to you is that time, in its unbroken commerce, should end by giving you an appearance, an external semblance, that is alien to your youth; and this may well affect you as a queer and irrevelant stroke. 'Sometimes,' said Edith, 'when I am dressing, I find myself wondering who is the ugly old woman using my glass.' It is a surprise—but too meaningless, too fortuitous, to be treated seriously. Whatever the years may have brought, whatever the pains and penalties of their private history, they are still the life you have always known, the old inseparable companion; and it is only in the glass that there is anything of a stranger in age.

'Only in the glass!' Even as I write the words I am checked by the thought of the change I should feel in the air, with no word spoken, if Edith were looking over my shoulder. I should be aware of a smile, and of something wry and dry in the smile, at my ignorance, my innocence, my lapse into convention and commonplace, with this fluent philosophy of the consolations of age. What do you think you know (says that smile) of the pains and penalties, as you call them, of a woman who was young and who grows old? It is pretty, this talk of saving one's youth for one's age, of enfolding the past in the present—and indeed it is a good thing to do if one can do it, for it passes the time and fills the day and keeps a playground open, with its cheerful noises, that would otherwise be shut. But thank you, it means more than you suggest, for all that, to see what it is that has changed, if only in the glass—'only' is an ingenuous touch! The pretty talk may begin to sound hollow. How about all that once hung on the youth that was *not* to be saved, which you let go so complacently? Do you think it wasn't much? Whatever it may have been, there was a time when it seemed a good deal—a time perhaps when it seemed to be all that made life worth living; and is this one of the quaint fancies, caught from the grimace of the glass, that are not to be seriously treated? Make no mistake: still to be able to live in your years with the young avidity and young audacity that you had and have kept, is all very well, and a power to be prized; but at the best it leaves you plenty of time to remember the things that you had and have lost—those trifles of young hope and young pride, filched by the way.— Enough, it is clear that much may be said in a smile; and it somewhat halts me, no doubt, in my smooth argument, my scheme of a life securely poised upon its rounded years. Yet I stick to my point, which is that the life I describe was one that drew towards age with a rare felicity, being a life that kept touch with its past. The easiest old age, of mellowest weather, is doubtless that which is sunned and soothed by indolence, placidly unmindful, lulling regret; but that was not for Edith. There is no such Indian summer of repose where a faithful memory, rather a grim servitor at times, is always on the watch with its offices of conscientious candour. No matter: if you wish for interesting entertainment in the fall of the year, not mere basking and dozing, the loyalest memory is the best companion, and the friendliest too in the end. As for Edith, if ever she winced at its plain speaking, she could also rest upon its friendliness in a mild and propitious hour. In such an hour we may see her, by a fortunate chance that gives the rightful close to this chapter.

There are moments [continues Madame de Divonne] in the story of a familiar friendship when it seems as though a page were quietly turned, almost unawares, bringing a fresh revelation of affinity to the light. So it happened to me one day with Edith, a day that stands out among the rest, as I look back, with an illumination of its own. I had gone to see her at St. Brice, and for once I found

her alone, without her usual encirclement, the barrier of duties and engagements, guests to be entertained, servants to be directed, by which she was
commonly enclosed and defended. I had arrived
early in the afternoon; it was a rainy day of autumn,
one of those days when the year seems to stand still
and time is endless. There was a delicious and un-
wonted sense of emptiness in the air, a pause in
which there was nothing to attend to, nothing to
do, but simply and solely to *be*. And so, as we sat
together in the quiet room, we *were*. Small cares
fell away and were forgotten—and it is the small
cares, not the great, that are a hindrance to communion between friends.

The hush of the hour could be seen in her face.
The restless beat of the eyelids which I knew so
well, as she looked about her for something amiss,
requiring her touch, was slackened and stilled; or
if there was a quiver it was only the track of a passing thought, a flicker of reflection. She forgot to
look for the flower to be straightened in the vase,
the cushion to be offered you, the little table to be
placed at your elbow; even Edith for the time was
content to *be*.

Presently, while the glow of the firelight shone
on the last roses of the year, the past was with
us in the room, summoned by Edith to join us—in
the form of an old scrap-book, in which, with a few
photographs, a series of newspaper cuttings, notices
and reviews of her first books, had been piously collected and pasted by her governess of early days,
till there were too many of them to be kept. Edith
turned the pages and showed me these relics with

fond amusement. I would sacrifice many a more eventful day, spent in her company, sooner than lose the memory of that hour. It was and still is a precious possession; I realised then, as never before, what Edith might have been for the children she never had. Most striking was the perfect simplicity with which she lingered over the record of the beginnings of her literary fame; she accepted her success without vanity and without false modesty, as a simple fact, as one accepts the heritage of one's race and blood. 'I began to write stories when I was four years old,' she told me, neither pluming herself nor belittling the gift; and it was the same throughout, as she dwelt serenely and impartially on her unfolding past—sensitive to its appeal, but without in any way heightening or dramatising it. She refused what La Fontaine calls 'le sombre plaisir d'un coeur mélancolique'; she regarded the days dead and gone with a smile of kindness, while she affectionately drew me in to share them with her. I discovered then, and have never forgotten, the warmth that was hidden beneath the cool surface of her being, as mountain flowers are kept warm by the protecting coverlet of snow.

It was a rare hour of revelation, soon past, and all the more to be prized for its rarity. I still see her pale hand as it turned the leaves of the album; it was like watching the dust of the past, dust with a glint of gold, stream between her fingers from page to page. Her work, her art, her fame, were the gold in it, and as the story grew the gleam absorbed it all. Sitting by her side, in the gracious and orderly room, with the rain beating and the leaves falling outside, I felt the presence of a power at rest, controlled by a lonely and generous spirit. It was a spirit that could take nothing from another, but it gave and gave to the end.

XIV

Last years, last thoughts

1

I cannot follow her further with any regularity—cannot and need not, for the design that was to be traced in this essay draws to its completion. She is in sight of seventy by this time; and with her eye for the seemly and befitting she liked to see herself a quiet stay-at-home by her fireside, reading her book, talking to a friend, while the world sped on its way without her. Let her take that view of herself by all means, a true view at certain times, so far as it goes. But it seldom went far, as those knew who saw her approaching and crossing the line of age. It was Edith on her feet in a moment, with new ideas in her head, new plans in her hand, Edith who could suffer no idle or unproductive moment in the day—it was she they had always seen and still saw much oftener than the other. What about Edith who, not content with her constant flights and excursions nearer home, had lately struck out on the largest of all her plans?—who had seized and chartered a ship with one hand, a bunch of choice companions with the other, and had sailed away to the isles of Greece and the realms of gold for a final great haul of impressions—to match that earlier draught, when once long ago she had measured the length of the Mediterranean and tilted the whole of it, as she said herself, into her gaping young mind. It was another and a more affluent mind that now received it, but still it was the same, as it threw itself wide to all the beauty that man so strangely bequeaths to memory in his death, in spite of his secular wreckage of it while he lives. But of that last Odyssey what word need be added to the three chapters where it is chronicled, that of its romance by Edith herself, those of its humour and its felicity by two of her shipmates,* which cut across each other to produce such a sharply lighted scene? Of another field of adventure, where it was not an Odyssey but a merry ring-time, often renewed, I should like indeed to tell more than I can; but the eyes were not granted me, nor are now to be supplied, for tracking her through later years in England, where her visits were a recurring descant on the main theme of the seasons, their regular swing between the winter of Sainte-Claire and the summer of St. Brice. She made more and more friends in England, among the native stock in their own wild garden, that was more than ever contrasted, in those loose-flying days between war and war, with her own mannerly parterre which nothing deranged. It was Edith descending as of old, stirring and illuminating the party she joined, gayest and vividest of guests—not without the old touch of royalty in her bearing, as of one who always arrives to find the hall door flung open, the carpet spread, the candles lighted on the stairs—but also Edith still holiday-making with her

* By Edith herself in *A Backward Glance*, by Logan Pearsall Smith, in *Unforgotten Years*, and by Mrs. Winthrop Chanler, in *Autumn in the Valley*.

engaging freedom; and Edith now conscious, I may dare to say, of possessing her ground, Edith more trustful of her instinct, as she passed to and fro among the islanders—a conclusion to be drawn from a significant little fact. She began to allow England, do you notice, to filter into her fiction—now and then, not obtrusively, till at last it was to be half of a wide-reaching novel, the novel by misfortune that she left behind her unfinished. It all makes me wish I could see more of her in England at that time; but I divine what I can.

On the other hand I am not left to guess the happy meaning of another affair, a flash of high light in these years—the occasion of her last return to her native land, after many years of absence. An unexpected call had determined it, and perhaps it would never otherwise have been made; but the call came, one that there could be no thought of resisting. 'I wonder whether you realise,' says G. L., prompting me, 'how enormously gratified she was by her doctorate at Yale'—and if I did not I easily believe it. Her visit, a very brief one, did not in fact do much to revive old memories or renew old ties, still less to start fresh discoveries; she couldn't, it seemed, cast herself with the impassioned curiosity of Henry James, for example, into the maze of the sensations of a 'restored absentee'; one short and somewhat flurried glance, and she was away again, pleased but distracted, evading the kindly pressure of many claims. Yet they were of deep import, the breathlessly numbered days. It was not that she was new to public and official awards of honour; her wartime work, and other works that arose from it, had brought her worthy and appropriate decorations. But these, well as she had earned them, she could not and would not prize as her own and none other's;

she was one of an army in what she had done to win them, and one of an army may justly be proud of a distinction, and yet it is not merely as his own that he wears it; he represents an army. This other was different; for when the University of Yale called her to accept the degree of Doctor of Letters it was a message to herself, to Edith Wharton the writer, and of writers there is happily no ranked army, but each is alone with his work, to answer for it; and what was more and a great deal more, the word came to her from her own country. Her degree was a symbol, and doubly so. The day when in cap and gown she stepped to receive it, smiling in dignity, was the pendant at this end of the years to the day when she had dashed up and down the stairs of her house in the first excitement of seeing herself in print; and so the story was balanced and completed as pictorially as the best of her own. That was much, but there was more. For however it was, and by now I have hardly to be particular in seeking the reasons, she had had through the years, mingled with many praises, no small portion of scolding in public from her critics at home—not all of it, she might think, fairly directed at her books, which were common property, but in part at matters of another kind, her slighting of what America offered, her preference for what Europe gave, which were her private affair; and if she seemed to be careless of the reproach (an additional offence!) it may after all have worn upon her patience and touched her sentience more than appeared; and to all this the resonant honour now accorded her at home, in so notable a quarter, was an answer on her behalf, the best, the only possible, in which she might well find a special satisfaction. But why worry at her feelings? She was enormously gratified, and had every right to be so. It seems a pity that she didn't linger a while in the fulness of the welcome that hailed her reappearance; but the heat was great, the friendly voices were bewildering in their multitude, her strength was not that of other days; and the Doctor of American Letters, waving her last good-bye to the land of her birth, sped back to her garden in Europe.

Here, as ever, her household of faithful friends was ready for her, the bodyguard devoted in service, with White the great and Gross the wise and tender at their head; they received her back into the fort they held for her against all the world.* It was just and right that the world should distinguish her, but crowned with her renown it was to them that she belonged, their possession and their pride. It was no light or facile art to which they were dedicated, the art of serving her as she would and should be served, but that was the greatness of it; they and they only had mastered it, they alone knew her demands and appreciated her due. It had needed close and intelligent study of her, but where was study more rewarding?—and it was a research in which there was no relaxing, no resting in the finish of perfection attained. Does the casual visitor suppose that even Edith must at times look in vain about her house for a flaw? They know better, who hear the punctual cry of her lament and reproach as she points it out. What of that?— for thus it is not only a creation of art and a labour of love, but her service is a drama of ever-living interest; and there is nothing humdrum, nothing monotonous in the administration of this trim city-state. It enfolded her on

* White was no longer in working command, but he was never out of sight, a supervising minister 'without portfolio.' Cook, the monumental chauffeur of other days, was unhappily a total loss, through a breakdown of health that had compelled his retirement.

her return from her excursions in the world, recovering its own. And for herself, it is easy to imagine what it was for her to find these outstretched arms of loyalty and affection at the end of all her journeys; here was safety again with these old friends—who knew her as few could, whose love for her was without a question, and who claimed her as their admired and treasured responsibility. A fortress and a city-state, do I say? But it had the warmth, the familiarity, the reassurance of a more intimate refuge, the nursery, when Gross, twinkling and smiling, with the joy of her welcome in all her wrinkles, was hugged by her child restored. This is Edith as she is seen with Gross, and as she is seen with no one else. And I perceive how it was that when in the course of nature the friends of her household began to fall and fail, she felt the loss of their supporting presence with a chill and pang of dismay that nothing else could strike into her life. Disaster from without may be dreadful, but it can be met and faced. It is when the ground quakes and yields beneath you where you stand, it is then you lose heart.

There was something else too that she found, not only devotion and protection for herself, among the guardians of her home—an interest, even an influence, that remarkably affected and pervaded her closing years. It had been a late and gradual infusion in her thought, and other currents had joined to increase it; but not the least of them, perhaps among the chief, was the constant presence beside her of a deep and simple, very simple but deeply fervent and true, illustration of religious faith. She may hardly have known how it began, but there came a change in the behaviour of her mind—as a glimpse some time ago suggested—

towards the obstinate conundrum of life's meaning, that had once seemed to be closed and disposed of for good and all. It had been closed by argument, but it was not by argument that it was reopened—rather by something that to her, so familiar with the use of discussion, might appeal with a stronger and stranger force. The two women who happened to be nearest her in the life of every day, beloved Gross herself, and Gross's deputy and successor in attendance, were women of devoutest piety: one of a piety all charity, like her selfless nature, the other of a nature and a fervour less tranquil, more exacting—both of them in diversity women in whom it was shown what religion may bring forth in a life, how enhance and how fill it, where the speech of reason has no concern. This is faith that is only to be known when you know it, only to be discovered when you see it— very different, it may seem, from faith that is expressible and discussible, that may be studied and appraised by report. A reasoned faith, addressing a critical mind, is estimable, not mysterious; it is surrounded by a margin of debate, where a critical mind is at home in exploration and works in an accustomed light. But faith that has nothing to say, faith that trims its lamp, kneels at the shrine and rises nourished, without a question to ask or to be answered—this has a silencing charm, a spell to impress, in which nothing is not strange to the judicial onlooker from without. Strange, alluring, and out of reach: for here, to such an observer, it is clear that there can be no attaining or acquiring it if you are without it; you have it or you have it not—and if not there is nothing you can do but only to acknowledge it when you see it, and to remember what you have seen. It is like the difference between the bravery that is conscious of danger, but gathers up its will and strains its nerve and still is brave, and the bravery that goes forward without a thought, needing none, for it knows no other way. Which of them is in reason the greater courage of the two? But we all know to which of the two our eyes turn.

Edith's home of safety could never again be the same when Gross was gone. But Gross was still beside her when a stranger appeared, one winter at Sainte-Claire, bringing other changes that in their kind were final. This was illness: not the illness that may drop in at any time in passing, to vex and harass and make what nuisance it can of itself till it passes on; she knew that one well enough, and had even had more than her share of it in younger days; not that, but the other kind, that which sooner or later comes with an unmistakable difference, with looks of deeper purpose and more deliberate intent. It may leave you good years still, as it left her not a few; but it stays thereafter within sight, ever on the watch. This was in 1929; she was sixty-seven, and her recovery was what is called complete; but she knew the warning, and it was plain that something had been thrown out of gear in her, something that showed in a slackening of the nerve and tautness of her self-command. Illness then, somewhere not far off henceforth: and also an entirely fresh acquaintance, never heard of before, mere money-trouble—not, I should say, in its fury, not crying havoc, but a disconcerting demon, playing its incalculable tricks on the amplitude of the use of money to which her hand had always hitherto been accustomed. She had made and she continued to make a plentiful income with her books; but the earnings of her books had been the loose change, so to speak, in her pocket, most enjoyable of coin, while her life and its structure stood fast on a solid plinth of 'private means'; and as for the fits and starts of private means, especially at that time of the American kind, their fallings from us, their vanishings, it is a story too dismal-trite to be dwelt on. These were anxieties, not perhaps very serious by most measures, and certainly not selfish; no one was less likely than she to be one of the rich who are personally affronted, as though by the bad manners of fortune, when they are constrained to be less rich than they were. The real shock, the profound and the irreparable—this came when Gross sank into a long last illness and memory left her, even the knowledge of her Edith, who could only place her gently in hands of ministering care till she sank out of life. And then, blow on blow, it was the illness and untimely death of the other and much younger of those two women, companions in her service—the one of whose attachment, and of whose miraculous divination (as it seemed to all who knew her) of Edith's needs and ways, Edith herself had not dreamt of ever having to face the loss. With the disappearance of these two she was left in a bewilderment of loneliness that was new and unknown to her; yet she was fortunate to have lived for so long before discovering what it is to be nobody's child.

And here, if to some it should seem that I have hitherto touched with an unfeeling hand a certain other tender strain in Edith's youth and age, I shall make amends with a quotation from two letters that she wrote, some years later and very near the end of her life, to one of the best and closest of all her younger friends, William Tyler.

Here I am [she writes from Sainte-Claire, April 16, 1937] desperately alone, for my little Linky died yesterday. She was ill only three days, and did not suffer. Her frail little organism was worn out. I wish she could have outlasted me, for I feel, for the very first time in my life, quite utterly alone and lonely.

And again, a month later:

During the last years of the Roman Empire the Emperors had a passion for human 'curiosities,' such as mermaids, fauns, centaurs, etc. There were professional collectors, and whenever one was found, he, she, or it was shipped to Rome (for they mostly came from Egypt or North Africa). Once they found a boy who *understood what the birds said;* and I have always been like that about dogs, ever since I was a baby. We really communicated with each other—and no one had such wise things to say as Linky.

2

I turn back to 1927, the year in which Walter Berry died in Paris; and here I may well pause in perplexity, wondering how I am to measure, how describe, the significance of this milestone in her story, now that it is reached. Walter Berry!—he comes forward again as he disappears, and comes in such a questionable shape that there is no letting him go without a parting demand, a call to deliver that has hung in the air unspoken through the years that we have watched. What are we to say of him as he goes, we to whom Edith was dear? Something was said on an earlier page, that looked forward; and now it is time, at this end of the tale, to ask what was left to her at last in return for all that she had entrusted to this friendship, this devotion that had polarised her existence for so long. How can we say, and is this not one of the questions I lately deprecated, which are not to be answered because the material for an answer is by the nature of the case unknowable? So it is in part, and the chiefest part—which is the balance of happiness and of pain in the memories that by now were piled so deep; only one thing is certain, that both were mixed in them, and another scarcely less so, that not happiness prevailed; and on this side the question is closed. Yet, if there is to be truth or validity in a portrait of her, it must be approached at another point, a more accessible, where the yield of this dominant and abiding preoccupation, and the worth of the yield, can in some sort be assayed. The question is here to be faced, and if I march straight up to it and say what strikes me first, it is this— that if ever there was a friendship that needed to be sunned and freshened by exposure to the light, to the breeze of the open, to the common influences of the weather, it was a friendship with that man; for whatever might be found of many kinds in what he brought to it, the springs of warmth and freshness would have to be sought elsewhere. Yes indeed, there was much of many kinds in what he brought—force of intelligence, weight of ability, wisdom of the world, well-stored knowledge and well-trained culture and all the rest of it; and with it all, exhausting the atmosphere that enclosed it, a perpetual leak of whatever gives to friendship its green leaf and its kindly flower. How else am I to put it?—and what more, what less, is honestly to be said? How or why an adventurous mind and a genial imagination should fall to be confided to such keeping is what nobody knows; but the thing done, it should be possible to see what becomes of them. As for the argument of her thought, and how it fared beneath the dry shadow of that ascendancy, I may leave what I have said; and now of the vision of her fancy—where it settled in its flight, once for all, on a chilly and insulated spot, that became an inviolable precinct—of this too some rueful account is to be taken. It is very sure that in such a case the imagination, poor creature, will find what it needs; for what it finds it will bend to its need, and there it is; or easier still, it will set itself to need what it finds. Anyhow it is satisfied; and in the case before us, as it happens, we needn't look far to discover what it was, the stuff of this enforced or this factitious satisfaction.

Look, then, at her books, and with a swift glance consider the assembly of men and women, of all ages and various conditions, who crowd the field of her twenty or thirty novels. A vigorous crowd it is, and among them are many, the most assured, the most confident of all in their reality, of whom you may ask where on earth, with her exclusive preferences, she had learnt to know them; but of course it was not on earth that she had known or had need to know them, she had divined them in flashes, in glimpses, keen and full enough for the curiosity, the brisk-eyed irony and humour of so busily creative a brain. There is no doubt about these unlikely strangers, from the humble and uncouth, with whom she had scarcely exchanged a word, to the voluble wretches, the gilded vulgarians, to whom her word had at most been of the curtest; firm on their feet, they live and grow in the shaping brain that had caught them in a flash. And then, of course, plenty of the people whom you would look to find in her company, clever and cultivated and civilised people, though at times they seem to be almost lost, a pale minority, among the louder and vivider sort; but still they are here, the men and women with whom she had actually lived and talked, who naturally could have no secrets from her, and the neatness of her discrimination, threading its way through their manners and motives, is no surprise. But look on still, in particular at the men, and single out one among them—not that I should say single him out, for he is several, with differing names and fortunes; but again and again he is the same in his variety, and he is one, and it is he I am after. How then, take him for all in all, shall I describe him? Calm and strong, a man of the world and of the best world, ripely experienced in the ways of the world and in the knowledge of men and women—especially women, for he is reported a man of powerful passions, with something of a stormy past behind him, stamp and guarantee of his authentic manliness; but master of himself and of his fate, a cool hand, a deliberate observer—so deliberate indeed that it is a wonder how he contains such fire and mettle within that impeccable front, or how his high composure could ever be touched by the loves and hates that rack our humanity. Will he never break down or flare up, never crash through his punctilio, never forget his manners? If one saw rather more, or heard rather less, of his virile and generous ardour, as he surveys the crowd with his superior air, it were a clearer case and a soldier form of a hero. But let him be. Long before this the worst has happened: a tap from a man of real bone beside him, any of a score in the jostle of the crowd, and this admirable

[228]

figure, this gracious mould of a man, is dead upon our hands, a shell, a simulacrum with nothing inside it to match the flesh and blood of its vulgar neighbour. That is what this novelist in all good faith has taken for a man, and in all seriousness has offered us as the flower of manhood. And whatever the effect of the fatality, critically speaking, upon the life of her books, the meaning I extract from it, the meaning to my purpose, is all too clear. Such is the doom of an imagination that alights on sterile ground, closes its wings and there resigns its freedom. Wherever it kept its freedom, which was everywhere else, imagination, agile and sensitive, worked its will, and worked it so well that the contrast was disaster for the luckless simulacrum. In short there was no food for a sharp-set fancy, only a stone, at the source where it accepted unquestioningly what it was given; and so it accepted the stone.

If I am to press more closely to what I mean, defining its edge, I might do so by leaving her books and confronting the two of them as they were—her, whom we know so well, and him, the only man who was not to be placed in the scale of mankind, to take his chance with the rest; and so he stood absolute and unrelated, where no light fell on him by reflection from others, for contrast or comparison. Suppose now that this man of privilege, with so many excellent possessions and acquisitions, is himself in his nature and proper being an image of convention all compact—of convention that studies the opinion of the world like its Bible, for that is its whole support, the staple of its life, however it may mask its dependence by airs of lofty disdain; for indeed, if you live on opinion, the sweetest savour is in the sight of opinion quaking a little, not only adoring, as you swallow it—quaking alarmed as well as fascinated by the authority, the mastery, the dignity, the breeding (especially the breeding) that is yours; but all this cautious planning could hardly be realised if it weren't for a deep vault of egotism within, spacious and cool, sealed against the variable currents of sympathy and humanity that may disturb the study and enjoyment of opinion; and it can't be helped if the chill from within pervades the outer climate, lowering the temperature of the life all round it, deadening its charm, cheapening its value. Picture, I say, all this—and then set before it, confronting it, a nature spontaneous in admiration, swift in interrogation, a bold and youthful and fun-loving spirit, which yet has excluded any view of this spectacle before it save one, one only and for ever. Here is a confusion of feeling and thought, now and ever, for that free spirit, free elsewhere. I have spoken of contradictions that were never resolved in her, a crossplay of impulse—straightness and frankness and tenderness that pulled against other forces which on their side were stiffly reluctant. Is that tug-of-war to be finally referred to this central antinomy, this everlasting attempt at an adjustment of incompatibles, the naturally free and the essentially bond? Not all of it, no doubt, for there were tough old restraints and suspicions that belonged to her heritage from the beginning; but the confusion I now speak of, disarraying the judgments of a clear mind and a generous heart, must have vastly contributed to the strains and stresses that were visible to the end. And I wonder, was she not conscious at last, or half-conscious, that this was the core of the trouble—that this paramount influence was not alone the inspiration she believed or was determined to believe it, but also a burden? No moment in life is stranger than that in which this discovery is made, if it is made; and if it is made after long years of belief in the inspiration, it may well be impossible to acknowledge it consciously; it is something which simply cannot be. And yet perhaps, when the end comes and the influence is removed, mingled with the dismay of the loss, the desolation of the sight of the empty place, there may be relief. There were those near her at the time who thought there was. And so that milestone is passed.

3

In the autumn of 1931 [writes Signorina Nicky Mariano], while paying one of her long visits to the Berensons at I Tatti, Edith Wharton suddenly proposed to me to come and spend a week with her in Rome. My first reaction, I confess, was against the idea. After first meeting her in 1923 I had again and again been a guest at Sainte-Claire, or had seen her as a guest of the Berenson household; I had had many proofs of her affection and felt real devotion for her. And yet the idea of a prolonged tête-à-tête with her filled me with a certain apprehension. She easily gave me on such occasions the sense of being 'weighed in the balance and found wanting,' as if I were not coming up to her expectations, and did not entertain and amuse her enough. A pleasant sense of intimacy or at least familiarity that I felt between us in the presence of others would suddenly disappear and leave me inwardly struggling to recapture it. However B. B. would not hear of such silly scruples on my part; he urged me to accept the invitation, and off we went, she, her beloved maid Elise, Linky, her little Pekinese dog, and myself.

My parents were not dog-fanciers, and in my grandmother's and brother-in-law's Baltic homes I had learnt to be very fond of huge Newfoundland dogs and other out-of-door pets. The lap-dog and its cult were a new experience for me, and already in the railway-carriage I found out that between Edith and her maid it formed a real bond and kept them happy and occupied. No danger of too much tête-à-tête as long as Linky was about.

Everything went off very well during the first days in Rome. Edith wanted particularly to see early Christian churches, and being fairly well prepared on that subject I made out various programs of sight-seeing, and they seemed to be just what she liked. The evenings were a little difficult, but all the rest developed so harmoniously that I did not mind them. We drove about in a taxi-cab, the oldest and dirtiest and most ramshackle cab in Rome, with a driver whose black coat had turned greenish with age. Even my not very violent national pride rebelled against this, and I asked Edith whether she would not like me to procure a car a little more in keeping with her station in life. She said no, she would stick to this man and engage him again, because he looked as if he would be kind to her little dog while we were inside a church. It was quite true: he was very tender with the little creature, and it gave me an insight into the quickness of her perceptions. She noticed details of expression and subtle nuances of mood in a flash, while apparently rather bored or otherwise preoccupied.

On the third day she asked me whether we had any chance of hearing some good church music, or at least of watching one of the more important religious functions. As it happened, the feast of the consecration of the churches of St. Peter and St. Paul was quite near, and I learnt that a pontifical mass would be sung by the Benedictine fathers at S. Paolo fuori le Mura in celebration of it. I expected a refusal from Edith on account of the rather early hour; but no, she accepted it with alacrity, and both she and her maid (a very pious Catholic, by the way) were ready before nine; so was the taxi-driver with the greenish coat, and we got there in good time. In the dim light of a muggy November morning the Basilica looked even vaster and emptier than usual; a small group of poorly clad parishioners from the *quartiere* S. Paolo was waiting before the central apse and watching the candles being lit by the sacristans. Never have I been present at a more magnificent and sumptuous and yet dignified and, I would almost say, severely classical ceremony, enhanced by the smallness and quietness of the congregation, which helped one to concentrate on what was going on in the apse. I felt deeply moved and at the same time acutely aware of Edith's presence— the presence not, as I had feared, of an impatient and rather spoilt woman, easily bored and anxious to move on, but of someone quite close to me, carried away with me and like me into another sphere, with no stiffness or impatience left in her, no

[233]

thought of the passing hour or of other plans. We stayed to the very end and followed the procession carrying the Blessed Sacrament all round the Basilica, until it had disappeared into the sacristy and the bell had stopped ringing and the candles had been put out.

That same day, at vesper hour, we went to St. Peter's, and watched the relics being shown there; and during the following days we assisted at various other functions and loved it all and felt in great sympathy; but the particular '*Stimmung*' of that dim November morning at S. Paolo never came back. It left me in the belief that Edith may perhaps have been much nearer to actual conversion to the Church than any of her friends ever thought. When I once told one of her *intimes* about this experience I found him sceptical. He admitted that she was very sensitive to the beauty of ritual, but could not imagine that there could be more than that in it. 'Anyway,' he said, 'if Edith should be converted to Catholicism, my heart would go out to her confessor!'

And yet I still believe that if the two humble and pious women near her and devoted to her, her maid and her housekeeper, had not died shortly afterwards and had continued to exert their mute influence over her, it might have happened and might have been a source of great happiness to her, helping her to let herself go more easily, and to let the soft and tender notes in her being be heard more clearly. Whenever in later years we happened to be alone together and I touched upon recollections of those Roman days, it brought an immediate response of sympathy from her, and even of wistfulness, as for something lost.

Something lost, something missed, or something found and discerned to be out of reach—which was it? Those who had known her from of old in tight possession of another doctrine, her brain swept clear of any cobweb of mystification, in all the severity of her rationality—it was natural for them, marking these signs of change, to take them as betokening a slipping and sliding of her assurance that could only end in one way, at one point of rest. Why should it not? A restless and desirous mind, increasingly aware that life had not satisfied its desire, and a mind instantly awake to beauty, that had made a strangely late discovery of beauty in a region overlooked hitherto—this was plain to see in her; and if a haven is revealed in which, when it is reached, peace is found, desire fulfilled, beauty attained, why shall it not be entered and occupied where it opens? The course might well seem clear; for if the old claims of reason, or what passed for it, have lost or are losing their sanctity in the revolution of your thought—or better, if reason itself now speaks another language—what else in the world should bar your way? Nothing, no doubt, if it were only a question of surrendering things that are in your right to resign—of changing the mind that is your own; if this were all, the choice is your own to make, the achievement of the reward is in your hand—difficult, painful perhaps, never impossible. It is not all. *Porro unum necessarium:* and this too, the last necessity, may to some be only the last and greatest difficulty; but to others, and I believe that Edith was one of them, it is impossible, and they have only to look straight at it to know that it is. Let those who best of all know the nature of the impossibility, for they have faced it and found it to be none for themselves, say what it was for her. 'It may have been,' says one, 'her deep respect for human excellence, coupled with the self-respect inseparable from it, that stood between her and the ultimate experience of the divine, which I think in a manner she coveted.' 'I think,' says another, 'that there was at the centre of her an irreducible *I myself* that would have made submission impossible for her.' Impossible, yes, because to her and to such as she the last necessity does not appear as a surrender and a submission, but as a betrayal. That self-respect, that *I myself*, if they seem to be yours to resign—well and good, they may go; but perhaps they wear another face, that of a trust that you have no title to refuse, a charge and a responsibility by which you are in honour bound. And what then? Those to whom that surrender is the highest of honour are the first to see that in the other issue it stands as a barrier insuperable. Those who see the crucial step before them not as a venture of faith but as a denial of faith— they must stay where they are.

But perhaps it is neither needful nor just to think of them as baffled pilgrims, disappointed of a hope, casting wistful looks at a refuge that is not for them. They have their own faith for their support; and if faith it is and they stand firm on it, there can be no regret and no empty-hearted longing in the regard that is absorbed and comforted by the distant beauty they descry— beauty which is for them as for all with eyes to see. Faith speaks to faith; and they who are brought to the discovery, late though it be, that the belief to which they hold, their certainty of the reality of beauty, is also and can only be their trust in a grace abounding, are not to be excluded from the converse of all the faithful by reason of the diversity, vast as it appears, in their recognition of the channel of grace. It is the channel, to take the words that have been given me, of 'respect for human excellence,' or it is the directer channel of 'experience of the divine'; no matter, somehow and somewhere they must join, if any faith at all is justified or any of the values that we find, within or without, are values indeed—things which reason cannot reckon or compute, only take (where it may not refuse them) on trust. I am reminded of a question-mark of Edith's, written in a common little copy-book that she somewhere acquired and that took her fancy with its stately imprint, *'quaderno d'uno studente';* it lay by her hand, and from time to time she would make a note in it, a remark to herself alone—not that she often talked to herself alone, but all the more these rare comments are touching in their sincerity. One day she wrote: 'I don't believe in God, but I do believe in His saints—and then?' It is with that question—'and then?'—that the 'unbeliever' takes his place among the congregation of the devout, assured for his part of his right to do so, in whatever conventicle may hold for him the value of beauty, the church of St. Paul Without the Walls or any other in the world; and he repels as equally wide of the mark the imputation of a mere esthetic self-indulgence, an idle trifling with a few pretty things to the slighting of their deep implications, and the compassion that sees him as vainly yearning for the consolation of the devout. Edith, I dare say, among the devout—and I say again of the simple kind, for the practice of a more sophisticated piety brought a much fainter appeal to her sympathy—found a freedom that was new to her and a comfort that she needed; and there could be neither in a tantalizing dream, if it were that and no more.

A friend of hers, one who knew her well and saw her often in these latter years, Sir Kenneth Clark, writes to me:

> I once pleased her by telling her that she was the only person I knew who seemed to understand with equal fulness both the protestant and the catholic mentality. She then told me that it had always been her ambition to write a novel of which the centre should be the conflict of these two impulses. It was on a drive to Beauvais, I remember, and all the way home she outlined the plot of the novel, which as usual she had remarkably clear in her head.

This perhaps says simply and plainly, with two words, what I have gone about to discover—though I am not suggesting that with the cloud of their associations they are simple words, especially when (as obviously here) they are taken in all the broader and none of the narrower of the meanings they will bear. Protestant and catholic: if the way is cleared for these two words and these only, there is no doubt which of the two was the word for Edith, first and last and always— for Edith and that *I myself* to which her loyalty clung; and well as she may have understood the other, it was with a projective and imaginative understanding, not of experience. There is something, it may be, a little dubious and dangerous in the attention of the protestant, where from his own independence he observes with deepening admiration the harmonious discipline of the catholic host. One of us may stand alone, and he must, but what of the rest?—is it not better for them, safer and wiser, to march in order? It is right for mankind (he may find himself thinking) to be mistrustful of its own sufficiency—right for all but a few; and even of the few there is but one for whom he can certainly vouch, which is himself. Well, if this is the conclusion it will not be for the first time that a refractory spirit is seen very protestant for itself, very catholic for the world of infirmer judgment. It is the temptation of the protestant, and let him tackle it as he may; and having done so let him do his best, as Edith for one did hers, to place himself with candour and fidelity in the mind of the catholic, esteeming the power and the glory that for the catholic is the fulfilment of submission. I was using the two words, I said, in the broadest of their senses, and of course it is still only in the broadest that I give one of them to Edith and leave her with it. But the other has now resumed its narrower meaning, at least its more familiar, with the sight of her absorbed in the latest and greatest of the concernments of her closing years—her diligent study of the doctrine and liturgy, the history and hierarchy, of the Catholic Church. It was to Sir Kenneth Clark that she bequeathed her library, and I learn from him that there is a larger collection of books in it on these and kindred matters than of any other single sort. So there it is. She learnt so much of the ancient faith as books could tell, and all that a mellowing judgment and a broadening sympathy could discern or divine. But it was not the faith for her; she was true to her own.

4

I should like if I might, for a last glimpse of her, or a last but one, to see her where she holds her place and rank as a writer, a novelist of America, by virtue of the long row of her books that was still lengthening year by year to the end. Not her rank in the vertical order, so to speak, of merit, not the place where her work will presently find its lasting level: that view of her, which time will show, I have purposely foreborne to anticipate. But in another aspect her position as a novelist, now and for the future, is already fixed by time and singularly visible; and that is the place in the line of her countrymen, companions of the craft, horizontally disposed, as I may say—where they file away as a procession into the past. It is the procession of American novelists from the beginning, wherever it began; and I suppose it would generally be said to have begun in earnest at Salem in New England and to have been headed by Nathaniel Hawthorne. I needn't try to count them as they follow in order; but when Hawthorne has passed, anxious and reserved, it is Howells, of cheerful and unfurrowed brow, who is conspicuous after him, and again a pace or two behind Howells the portlier presence of Henry James; and these three are enough to give its character to the procession and to mark the curve of its course. They and the others between and among them make a various company, but it is compact in its formation—save for a straggler or two, skirmishing outside their ranks—and of kindred demeanour; and this for the reason that these Americans—none the less American because many of their books, and many of the weightiest, came to birth under other skies—were still of Europe in their art, and in much more than their art, in the climate of their culture, in the style and habit of their thought. On whichever side of the ocean they lived and wrote it was their affiliation with Europe that set their tone, in living and in criticising life, and their United States, apart once more from the very few roving adventurers of the 'frontier,' were those that faced the Atlantic; and even the most home-keeping of them could always see Europe in the distance—with frowns or smiles as might happen, with stern or benevolent regards, but they never lost sight of it. Whether or no it was a necessary condition for their work in their time—and there was evidently some debate among them on the point, doubts and self-questionings—it was a condition implicitly accepted; they had no thought of a declaration of independence, to set the Union free to fare ahead by itself and to live on its own resources. Much has come to pass since then—not merely a declaration of independence, but a 'Boston tea-party' of the liveliest, not to say the most uproarious, and a casting overboard of the wares of the old world that was little prefigured in the splash of the historic chests. And so the 'American school' of fiction, having made its clearance, comes in like a lion; and the earlier procession, with Hawthorne at its head (Hawthorne, shall we say, scared by the distant roaring, or proud of it?—something of both), winds off in its completeness, an illustrious body, united in their order for all their disparity, marching in honour and sobriety—not roaring at all.

It is at the end of their line, the last of the departing troop, that I see Edith Wharton; and a bright finish she gives to it, a trick of gay colour at the tip of its tail. I can even imagine that some of the company, turning to observe her, might eye the plume of her mundanity with suspicion. Is Hawthorne to believe that such a denizen of an irresponsible world is really what she so little appears, a serious writer, a working woman of letters?— and moreover, American-born if she is, how comes so frank and unashamed an apostate, for such he must deem her, to be enrolled in his succession? As for the first question we know that he may be reassured, and that there was nothing unprofessional in her application and addiction to her craft; his own was no deeper in its sincerity. And as for the second—but this, to my thinking, arouses a larger and wilder surmise. Hawthorne, to be sure, is easily answered again; if he allows New York to be America, the stamp of her nativity is still what it was at the beginning, beyond dispute or mistake; if he had seen her in Europe, as we have, he would own her his inalienable compatriot. The finer question, I am inclined to say, is whether she actually was not a great deal more American still, and whether the right field for her art, if she could have believed it, would not have been the most native of all, the furthest from all sight and thought of Europe. For such an idea she gave more than one suggestive occasion in the course of her work, as has widely been remarked. Indeed she grew tired of being told, she heard it so often, that the height and crest of her achievement was a certain little tale, a wonder of insight and divination, in which she completely turned her back on the scenes of her origin and nurture; and she might be impatient of the ingeminated cry, but the fact remains that in *Ethan Frome*—and perhaps even more elsewhere, whenever she faced the rawness of the 'frontier,' geographical or moral—it is somehow,

[242]

against all likelihood, as though she came home to her own; for here, as it seemed, she found herself in contact with people and things that spoke up and answered to the most original, the most spontaneous of the souls within her—that of the lurking adventurer, who saw more clearly and felt more keenly and understood with a greater relish of appreciation the drama of the wilds, among the hewers of history in the making, than ever the genteel play, in an ordered enclosure, of a company living on such history as it possessed, unearned at that. Change places, as the mad king said, shuffle the parts, and handy-dandy, a novelist of the best society is at large in the open, a laughing explorer, thoroughly enjoying her freedom. Was she really made for the politer world—where her ease was never complete, where her guard was never dropped, where her situation had always to be thought of and cared for and even rather sharply insisted on? At the end of all I could doubt it.

But that is a dream. She follows in the train of the old school, sure enough, where all the influences of her birth, all the fortunes of her life, were combined to place and to keep her; and a lingering look may dwell on the picture that she makes as she goes. And then inevitably my eye moves on to the massive figure in front of her, as she edges her way to his side with a light familiar blow upon his shoulder, and they fall once more into their interrupted talk. It carries me back to the old days, when she was first seen in his company—the days when she seemed to him, with her 'case' so consummately treated, as good as a novel of his own. And now he could see how the case had been wrought to a yet more masterly perfection; it was but a first light sketch that he had admired long ago. Her own little literary talent, pretty as it was, had struck him as almost an irrelevance in those days, a hardly needful decoration of a design so happily conceived without it. But here it is now an integral part of the subject, deliciously complicating it, worthily tasking and straining the art that clothes it in form. The novel in Edith Wharton!—by this time it matches his best, a creation of his latest manner. The *faisan d'or,* with her brilliant plumage, had charged into the purlieus of the toilers, a lovely and disturbing apparition; but that so far is nothing—they do it all the time, the fair intruders, on fire to be seriously received as artists, heaven help us!—and an amusing story may be made of it if you please, but it is a trifle; and they soon float back to the azure sphere where they belong. Here was something very different: she actually grasped what she was about, this one, as she settled down to her work and stuck to it; and on fire as she was with her ambition, her head was cool, she knew her place, and her pride in it was as sound as her modesty. The sagest and sternest of the craftsmen must admit that she meets them on their ground, and they must reckon with her; not she is to be smiled at and waved away to her playmates in the world—nor she to be caressed and courted (this also is a sight that has been seen in the workaday barnyard) for the heavenly radiance that is shed on the homelier stock by her presence. In short, concludes the master, she is one of us; and yet, bless her, she is always the golden pheasant as well, and she can't help it; and she is just as much bent on the pursuit of perfection in that part as in the other, making the most of it that can be made, making an undeniably finished and exquisite thing of it too. And if this doesn't all work up into a decorate intricacy of picture and drama, a masterpiece of intertwined refinements!—a very Golden Bowl of a pheasant, if the daring figure be allowed. There they are then, he and she, together again. They always enjoyed talking to each other so much that they enjoyed it more than reading each other's books; and they disappear over the hill, at their end of the winding line, still talking. A blessing on them both from all who are left to remember the great cause they have to miss them.

5

It was in the spring of 1937, at Sainte-Claire, that illness struck again and struck mortally, though there were still a few months of partial recovery before the end, and she was able to make her usual migration before the Provençal summer and to reach the Pavillon Colombe in time for the flowering of her northern garden. But there was little strength left in her, and she gratefully surrendered herself to the care of her attentive friend, Mrs. Royall Tyler, who had arrived to watch over her and who remained with her to the last. Another friend whom we know, Madame Saint-René Taillandier, finishes her recollections with a moving glimpse of her, a sight familiar and new—Edith among her flowers, Edith with her loosening hand on life.

I had heard, returning from America, that she was dangerously ill. One day in July Mrs. Tyler made me a sign: Come, you will see her; and I knew what it meant. And so I saw her once more. She joined us after the meal—her old self in appearance as she came towards me, smiling her welcome, in a soft grey dress, neat and elegant as ever.

'Oh I'm so glad you could come,' she said; and I could almost have thought her recovered, had I not been conscious of the vigilant anxiety of her friend and her attendants. She drew me into the library for a talk, curled herself up with her pretty feet (her *pieds de biche* as we called them) in the depths of the grey sofa, and asked about my travels. But after a few minutes, on a pretext confided to me beforehand, our semblance of a conversation was interrupted, and the rest of my visit was spent in the garden. A servant pushed her wheel-chair, and she set forth to examine her roses, carefully and seriously as in other days; we followed three paces behind, that she might not exert herself to talk. Silently she held out a rose to me; I took it and kept it, knowing it to be the last good-bye; a wave of the hand, and I left her. Ten days later she was gone.

A cluster of old friends assembled round her grave in the Cimetière des Gouards at Versailles, and after the service the hymn 'O Paradise, O Paradise' was sung by her wish. She had also chosen the words that were later set upon her headstone, a marble cross—*O crux spes unica*. However she interpreted the words, and whatever the hope she discovered in them, they are the last to be heard of the thoughts that were deepest in her mind. Her grave is next to that of the man whom she had loved for a lifetime, in youth and age.

Index

INDEX